Too Good to be True

Too Good to be True: Trauma Drama~Breaking the Cycle

Aaminah "QueenX" Dark

Royalty Retreatment Publishing

Too Good to be True:
Trauma Drama-Breaking the Cycle
Copyright © 2020 Aaminah "QueenX" Dark

ISBN: 978-1-7363179-0-7 (Paperback)

Cover design: Nitelite_studio

Printed in the United States of America.

First printing edition 2020.

Royalty Retreatment Publishing
PO Box 23261
Phoenix, Az 85063

www.royaltyretreatment.com

About the Author

Aaminah "Queen" Dark was born and raised in Philadelphia, Pennsylvania. Haunted by her own life experiences and affected by the experiences of others, she developed a passion for healing and growth. Since her discovery of trauma, Aaminah has acquired a second Master's degree, a post Master's certification, and attended several trainings to grow her knowledge and understanding of the topic. The most impactful training she participated in, was Dr. Bruce Perry's NMT (neurosequential model of therapeutics) training for children who have experienced trauma. She is currently on her way to becoming a certified trauma trainer. Her ultimate goal is to help the Black man and woman rebuild the Black family and restore the Black community.

If unconditional love was a person

I Love You
"Dawnie Special"

Dedications

First, I dedicate this book to my father. For not only influencing the character, morals, and values that make me who I am today, but for always saying "You need to write a book. You have something to say that others need to hear."

Thank you, Daddy.

My second dedication goes to some very special men in my life whose presence and/or words spoke volumes. My brother Karim, My Uncle Ed, My Uncle Buzz, and two of my closest friends, Joel and Buckz.

Thank You.

My last dedication goes to everyone else; for I have learned many lessons from you all. Whether directly or indirectly. Whether positive or negative.

Lesson Learned.

Contents

Introduction

My mind wonders if true love really exists. A
feeling that hangs in the midst of a crowd I catch a
glimpse. Trying to grab for it but it slips, through
my fingertips. Leaving me with the desire for it, but
its swiftness makes me wants to quit.

-QueenX

As a child, one of my greatest fears was
ending up old, miserable, and alone.
Although I was never desperate to be in a relationship, when the relationships I was in didn't
work out, my fear would intensify. Also, whenever someone I knew experienced a break-up or

divorce, their failed relationships would also contribute to my fears. Just like most of you, I wasn't surrounded by many relationships. In fact, most of the relationships I was exposed to were extremely unhealthy. I had no-one to talk to about what it means to be in a healthy relationship, and how to build one that was long-lasting. At the time, I didn't realize it, but this fear sparked my desire to figure out why relationships fail and how to establish and maintain a healthy relationship in order to avoid loneliness in the future.

In 2005, I began my undergraduate studies as a step towards discovery. After 15 years, I have acquired a Master's degree in Forensic Psychology, a second Master's in School Counseling, and a Post Master's Certification in Child and Family Therapy. With my collective education, training, and research; and my decade of experience in mental health and counseling, I recognize the single source that plagues the relationships within the Black community.

Some of you may be aware, and some may not, but unresolved trauma has destroyed the Black family over the course of generations, and it will continue to do so if the cycle is not broken. Now, when I speak of unresolved trauma, I am not only referring to the personal traumas that have occurred in one's life, but the historically traumas that have affected the Black lineage as well. My interest in learning about trauma, was due to meeting a guy whose life had been so unfortunate, that establishing close healthy relationships was basically impossible. The effects of his traumas were so severe, that he would become overwhelmed with fear and doubt; eventually, he would end up sabotaging his relationships. The worst part about it, he didn't even realize he was doing it. It was at this moment that I thought to myself; if his own lifetime of traumas can affect his ability to trust and be in a relationship, how then can 400 plus years of trauma not have an even more severe impact on Black people as a whole?

This question led to my research, where I was introduced to Dr. Joy DeGruy, the author of "Post Traumatic Slave Syndrome." I used her findings and other research to help identify and discuss the "why" behind the problems between Black men and Black women. Normally, when asked about their opinions regarding the problems within their relationships, most times the women blame men and vice versa. Both, of course, have valid points, but none leading to any solutions.

What's interesting about this book, is that when collecting data to help guide this process, only Black men, ages 24-53 were surveyed. This doesn't mean that the voice of the Black woman isn't important, it simply means that as Black women try to manifest a healthy relationship with Black men, their thoughts, feelings, and experiences need to be heard. Another reason Black men are more of the focus in certain parts of this book, is because the issues of mental health is mostly a female-dominated discussion. Black men either don't participate in the conversation (for fear of it being used against them later), and when they do, it's only a few voices and they aren't really heard.

One of the things I found interesting when reviewing the data was the use of the word "good." The phrases "I'm a good man" or "I want a good woman" was used, but not simultaneously with being healthy. Within this book, the idea of being healthy is the overall focus; so, I would like to challenge you to use the term "healthy" instead of "good." "I'm a healthy Black man" or "I want a healthy Black woman." "Good" is having the qualities required for a particular role and being morally right. Mentally healthy is the ability to learn, feel, express, and manage a range of positive and negative emotions. It is also the ability to form and maintain good relationships with others. Essentially, a good person can exist and not be healthy, but a healthy person cannot exist without being good. This understanding will not only allow you to distinguish between healthy and unhealthy characteristic traits within yourself and others, but also the healthy and unhealthy ways to deal with conflict and uncomfortable emotions within your relationships.

In order to really identify effective solutions, the unhealthy characteristics traits and reactions to conflicts needed to be researched and discussed. Not only does this book examine the historically traumas that impact both, it also addresses the impact of personal traumas as well. Trauma is acknowledged and analyzed to help explain how it impacts the brain's stress response system, and how that connects to your thoughts, feelings, and behaviors within relationships throughout your lifetime. Ensuring you connect the dots between your past and present is essential when moving to a place of healing.

Healing seems to be one of those words that is thrown around because it sounds good. When scrolling through Facebook, you'll occasionally see a shared post that says "You can't heal if you're pretending, you're not hurt," or "I'm taking this time to heal so the next person gets the best version of me." So many people like and share these posts, but how many are actually holding true to what they are liking and sharing? How many want to hold true to what they are liking and sharing, but don't know how? Although healing is easier said than done; it's important every person gets to this place in order to succeed. "If you don't heal what hurt you, you'll bleed on people who didn't cut you." Even though your traumas are not your fault, your healing is your responsibility.

There are five goals I intend to accomplish in this book. The first goal is to help you recognize the connection between your historical and personal traumas and the distress you experience in your current relationships. The second goal is to help you to identify the healthy and unhealthy characteristics traits within yourself and others. The third goal is to help you regain control over your life and achieve healing by learning and using the skills of resilience and the phases of recovery. The fourth goal is to help you learn and use the concepts for dating with a purpose. Lastly, to help the black man and woman reconnect and rebuild the black family. Building upon these skills in ways that will not only positively impact your present, but your future descendants is essential. Let's focus on rebuilding what this country has strategically destroyed over the course of generations.

U. N. I. Together.

-Queen

Part I: The Black Woman

Angry Black Woman

Why do Black Men ask…
Why are Black Women
so Angry?
As if we didn't collectively experience
400+ years of slavery

Being tortured, beaten and
raped
Wishing to be saved
Then later being forced to bear,
for the white man
Yet another slave

But not just any slave, a house
nigger slave
You know light skin, long hair
Seen as better in those days

Oh Wait…ain't shit changed.
Except now, a lot of Black men
think the same.

Why are Black Women
so Angry?

I don't know
Maybe from having our babies
kidnapped, sold and killed
Or
being given to the master
to be raped at his will
And worse, through it all
have some Black men be still

Why are Black Women
so Angry?

Maybe due to drug infestation
and mass incarceration
Leaving Black women to lead
the household alone
For what seems to be an endless
duration

Why are Black Women
so Angry?

Maybe due to being fatherless
Leading to feeling worthless and
powerless
against the powers that be

Instead of being loved,
protected and valued…
unapologetically

Why are Black Women
so Angry?

Maybe due to the fear of being
old and alone
Especially when our Black men
become successful
And make a white woman his
backbone

Why are Black Women
so Angry?

Maybe due to being the most
disrespected and unprotected
woman in this country
Despite being the heart of the
Black community

Black Men
PLEASE STOP asking
Why are Black Women
so Angry?

It dismisses our experiences and
creates feelings of devalue
Instead, the question you should
be asking is
Why the fuck ya'll ain't angry
too?

QueenX
10/12/2019

Chapter 1: Where it all Began

For hundreds of years, the Black family has been under attack. This country has worked to ensure that not only is the Black man absent from the home, but if he is present, the Black man and woman are at odds. Today proves that all the hard work this country has put in has paid off; the divide is real and for so many different reasons.

So, what's the solution? In order for a problem to be solved, you must first identify the cause(s). The same applies to resolving the problems between the Black man and woman. To do this, we have to go back to where it all began.

The Independent Black Woman

In 1712, a man named Willie Lynch was said to have given a speech on the bank of the James River in the colony of Virginia on The Making of a Slave. Although his existence has been up for debate, the process of the Making of a Slave holds true. "Let's Make a Slave" is a study of the scientific process of man-breaking and slave-making, which required a Black man, a Black pregnant woman, and a Black male offspring. It was reported that W.L began the speech by highlighting the reason for his presence.

"I caught the whiff of a dead slave hanging from a tree, a couple miles back. You are not only losing valuable stock by hangings; you are having uprisings and slaves are running away. I have a full proof method for controlling your Black slaves. I guarantee every one of you that, if installed correctly, it will control your slaves for at least 300 years." The first two strategies given, were called the cardinal principle for making a

Negro and the breaking process of the African Woman.

It was believed that the cardinal principle for making a male slave is to "Keep the Body, Take the Mind." In other words, "break the will to resist; which is similar to the breaking process of a horse." Because the goal was long-range economics, he said, "You must keep your eye and thoughts on the female and the offspring. If you break the mother, she will break the offspring." The breaking process of the Black woman began first with forcing her to watch, along with the other Black men, the strongest and meanest Black man being stripped, tar/feathered, set afire and pulled apart by horses. The next step was having her watch the remaining Black men being bullwhipped almost to the point of death. Due to the trauma of her being left alone, unprotected, and with the Black male image destroyed, her psychological state moved from being dependent on the Black man to a frozen state of independence.

It was stressed that in this frozen state of psychologically independence (without the influence of the Black man), she will fear for the life of her male offspring and raise her female and male off-spring in reverse. She will psychologically train her male offspring to be mentally weak and dependent, but physically strong and her female offspring to be psychologically independent. In the end, you will have generations of Black women out in front and Black men behind and scared.

A few centuries later, between the 1970's and the 1990's, the Black community was hit with yet another strategic attack orchestrated by the United States government. One of the biggest attacks that contributed to the independent woman mindset among Black women, was the mass incarceration of Black men. The "war on crime" began from Lyndon B. Johnson's statement that "the Black community pathology caused poverty and crime."

During Nixon's administration, he declared a "war on drugs" and justified it with speeches about being "tough on crime." Although the prison population began to grow under his presidency, it truly exploded during Ronald Reagan's administration. When Reagan took office in 1981, the total prison population was 329,821. In 1982, he declared a "war on drugs and when he left office in 1989, the prison population had essentially doubled, to 627,588. This unbelievable rise in incarceration hit the Black community the hardest.

The 13th amendment says Neither slavery nor involuntary servitude shall exist within the United States, or any place subject to their jurisdiction <u>except as a punishment for crime</u>. So, essentially, mass incarceration is modern-day slavery. Just like the goal was to remove the Black man from the Black family on the plantation, the goal now, is to remove the Black man from the home through incarceration.

By continuing the strategic removal of the Black man, the psychological state of the Black woman continues to be frozen in a state of independence. Just like it was foretold, "In the end, you will have generations of Black women out front (head of the house) and Black men behind and scared."

The Angry Black Woman

> *"They get mad. They get angry. You see a lot of sisters go, 'You fuck with this kind of girl and that kind of girl? That shit is exotic! That shit look a lot different than the shit you see in*

the neighborhood all of the time. That shit look like it came off a boat. It feels like something that you can't just get and it's interesting to explore. But they get mad. They get angry."

-50 Cent

"They get mad. They get angry"

The audacity of this boy. As if a Black woman's womb didn't give him life. But unfortunately, this is a conversation we have to have all too often because of the angry Black woman comment coming from both Black men and non-Black people. Black women are constantly labeled angry, but not just because we actually express anger, which humans are allowed to do by the way. A Black woman is called angry when she speaks passionately about something, when she is direct and clear about who she is, and what she wants, or when she just speaks her minds in general, even when using a soft tone. Let's be real; a Black woman who speaks out equals being angry.

Where in the hell did the phrase "Angry Black Woman" come from anyway? How did such a natural emotion become such an excessively toxic label for a Black woman? The answer; another strategic attack by white supremacy. Thanks to the character Sapphire, the angry Black woman was born. Sapphire Stevens, in the TV show Amos 'n' Andy, was portrayed as a loud, stubborn, and overbearing woman who emasculated Black men. She was bitter, unhappy, mean spirited, and abusive. It was said that although Black men were the primary target, she had venom for anyone who insulted or disrespected her.

There was an episode in the show where Sapphire's mother displayed the same behavior. The episode begins with her husband, George, being worried because she had disappeared. It was soon revealed that, under the direction of her mother, she left her husband abruptly and was instructed not to return nor tell him her whereabouts. "It's the only way to bring that bum to his senses. And you're going to stay away from him until he finds a job and makes up his mind to support you." Even though Sapphire didn't like running off, she complied.

According to an article written in the Iowa Law Review, this so-called "Angry Black Woman" is the physical embodiment of some of the most negative stereotypes of Black women. Some of those stereotypes are out of control, disagreeable, overly aggressive, physically threatening, loud, and to be feared. She will not "stay in her place." She is not human. Although Amos 'n' Andy, birthed and perpetuated the stereotype of the angry Black woman, it did not stop there.

Hollywood is known for constantly portraying this cinematic stereotype. Black women are commonly portrayed as neck-rolling, finger-pointing attitude-filled women, who no man desires. Some of the most historical angry Black woman characters are Aunt Ester from *Sanford and Son*, Willona Woods from *Good Times,* and Florence Johnston from *The Jefferson's*. Some of the most current characters would be Rochelle Rock from *Everybody Hates Chris,* Clarice Johnson from *Not Easily Broken,* and the infamous Angela Williams from *Why Did I Get Married*.

The power of images dominates the mind more than we realize, and the continued exposure to these stereotypical representations of Black women has hugely affected the way Black women are viewed as a whole. Are there Black women that fit the angry Black woman description? Yes. But are there also a ton of Black women who don't? Yes. Unfortunately, it seems as though, no-one can tell the difference or they strategically use the term angry to diminish the value of what you are saying or doing to make themselves feel better.

For example, Serena Williams is the greatest tennis player of all time. During the 2018 US Open, she was penalized for "verbally abusing" the umpire because she said "You took a point from me...you're a thief and you owe me an apology." She explained that men have said a lot worse and have never been penalized. She felt the chair umpire was being biased, and she was correct. Serena was not being verbally abusive, she was simply expressing how she felt about the unfair calls the umpire was making, which was affecting something extremely important to her. Had she been white or a man, she would not have been penalized in the same manner. Since Serena is a woman, she was penalized because she didn't portray ladylike behaviors during the match, especially when addressing a white man. Coupled with the fact that she's a dark-skinned Black woman, she's not just unladylike, but loud, angry, and out of control - the angry Black woman.

Serena is not alone, there are tons of Black women who either get penalized for speaking their minds or suffer silently from holding in their frustrations. So many Black women feel pressured to conform to their environments in order to avoid the angry Black woman label, while others have given up on trying to appease people. They believe they don't get taken seriously, and/or it doesn't matter what a Black woman says or does, she will always be seen as angry.

"That shit is exotic!"

Comments such as this create feelings of anger within Black women. The idea that in order for a woman to be exotic, she has to be anything but what "looks" Black is preposterous. This is a clear example of colorism. A prejudice or discrimination based on the relative lightness or darkness of the skin; generally, within the same ethnic group. Without a doubt, colorism is and has always been a huge emotional and psychological problem within the Black community. So much so, that Black women and young girls see no value in themselves unless they exhibit "white features"; light skin, narrow nose and long straight hair.

The concept of light versus dark, within the Black community, started with the raping of Black women during slavery. When Black women would give birth to mixed babies, the complexion of those children eventually created a new status for the Black slave. These statuses were called the house negro and the field negro. The field negro worked in the field, slept in the barn, ate poorly, had an unclean hygiene, and was horribly mistreated. The house negro work in the house, slept in the basement or attic, ate what was left of the master's meal, had better hygiene and clothing, and was still mistreated, but not as bad as the field negro.

After a while, this new slave status developed a series of tests that determined if a Black person warranted "inclusion." These tests were called the ruler test, the snow and blow test, and the infamous brown paper bag test. The ruler test was used to determine if your hair was straight or not. If your hair was as straight as a ruler, then you passed the test. The snow and blow test was used to analyze one's hair and complexion. If your skin was white as snow and your hair blew in the wind, then you passed the test. The last test was the brown paper bag test, and this test was solely complexion-based. If your skin was lighter than a brown paper bag, then you passed the test. If you passed any of these tests, you were then considered, beautiful, smart, better, and worthy.

What makes the brown paper bag test so infamous, is the fact that this test is what created the internalized racism that exists within the Black community today. Black people adopted this test and began using it to exclude their own people based on the darkness of their skin. New Orleans invented the brown paper bag party, and if you were darker than the brown paper bag, then you were not allowed into the party. Black churches would hang a brown paper bag up outside the front doors and if you were darker than the bag, then you weren't allowed in. And sadly, some HBCUs would use this test to determine eligibility for admissions into the school, as well as admissions into Black fraternities and sororities.

The brown paper bag test also made its way into the minds of Black youth. In 1940, Kenneth and Maime Clark conducted a doll experiment to investigate the self-perception, of a Black child, as it relates to race. The experiment looked at children, ages 3-7, in mixed schools in the North in comparison to segregated schools in the South. The children were brought into a schoolroom one by one, and presented with 4 dolls (two shades of white and two shades of black). Each child was asked the same series of questions regarding the doll.

1. Which doll would you rather play with?
2. Which doll is the nice doll?
3. Which doll looks bad?
4. Which doll has a nice color?

The percentage of Black children who preferred the white doll, was 72% for the North, and 62% for the South. The percentage of Black children who said the white doll was nice, was 68% for the North, and 52% for the South. The percentage of Black children who said the Black doll looks bad, was 71% for the North, and 49% for the South. And the percentage of Black children who said the white doll had a nice color, was 63% for the North, and 57% for the South.

In the end, it was found, that Black children saw, and thought less of themselves, when compared to their white peers. From their own mouths, they preferred the white doll because "He's pretty" and rejected the Black doll because "he's ugly" or "he got black on him." The most devastating part of this experiment was when the children were asked to self-identify with one of the dolls. When asked to do so, some children resulted to humor and rationalization to cope with identifying with the "bad" and "ugly" doll. One child said, "He looks bad cause he hasn't got a lash," and another child said, "I'm white. I look brown because I got a suntan in the summer time." Other children, who were unable to cope with identifying with the Black doll, broke down crying. Two children ran out of the room, unconsolably convulsed in tears.

The concept of light skin being better than dark skin didn't stop there. It wouldn't be America without the media and Hollywood using it as propaganda to continue the conditioning of Black people, and deepening their internalized racism. In 1990, the hit show, "The Fresh Prince of Bel Air" aired with Janet Hubert playing Aunt Viv. In 1994, Janet Hubert didn't return to the show. Instead of replacing Janet with a woman that resembled her, she was replaced with a light skin Daphne Reid. When the differences between both Aunt Viv's were discussed, it was said that "the first Aunt Vivian had a much stronger and more confident disposition. The second Aunt Vivian came across as a far more non-confrontational woman, especially when it comes to her marriage."

In 1992, the hit show, "Martin" aired with the dynamic duo, Pam and Gina, played by Tichina

Arnold and Tisha Campbell. Gina was light skin, worked at a public relations firm, in a steady relationship with Martin, and was spared the constant insults and animal jokes. Pam, however, was considered Gina's subordinate at the PR firm. She was always the butt of insulting jokes from Martin, she never had a steady relationship, and she portrayed the negative stereotypes of the angry black woman; loud and aggressive.

In 2001, the hit show, "My Wife and Kids" aired starring Jazz Raycole as Claire. Jazz played Claire for the first season, then she was removed from the show by her mother due to a pregnancy storyline that she didn't agree with. In the second season, Jazz was replaced by Jennifer Freedman for the duration of the show. Same as with the Aunt Viv character, Jazz was not replaced with a girl that resembled her; dark skin with natural hair. Instead, she was replaced by a light skin girl with very long and curly hair.

Believe it or not, the brown paper bag test still exists today. It has since transitioned into Black people promoting a light skin versus dark skin party. P. Diddy putting out a Cîroc promo flyer asking for White, Hispanic, and light-skinned Black women only. Chris Brown banning "darkies" from his section in the club and "only f**king with black b***hes with nice hair." Omarion stating that he only dates light skin women. L'Oréal lightening Beyonce's skin to sell a product. 50 Cent calling non-black women exotic and all the black men that either have been or are married to white women; such as Taye Diggs, Terrance Howard, Omari Hardwick, and Cuba Gooding Junior.

The "independent" and "angry" Black woman are products of socially constructed tactics used to destroy the Black family and community. First, by attacking the mind of the Black woman, which was done by depriving her of the Black man and destroying his image in the process. Second, by destroying the image of the Black woman in the eyes of the Black man. Consequently, over the course of generations, media propaganda, colorism, and the strategic removal of the Black man from the home, has fed the mindset of the independent/angry Black woman. Ultimately, this pattern creates the non-preferred woman that exists today.

Processing Session

1. Were you aware of the Making of a Slave process?
2. How does the process of the Making of a Slave make you feel?
3. Now that you understand the slave making process, explain how that process is relevant today.
4. Knowing the purpose of the Making of a Slave process, how will you move forward with ensuring that who you are is not the person America intended to make?
5. Have you ever been referred to or referred to a woman as the Angry Black Woman? How did you/she respond?
6. Ladies, have you ever found yourself adjusting who you are in an attempt to avoid the Angry Black Woman label? What exactly did you do? How did you feel afterwards?
7. Fellas, knowing how the Angry Black Woman label began and why it was created, how will you move forward with ensuring you aren't perpetuating the stereotype created to destroy the Black woman?

8. Ladies, have you ever been a victim of or enabler of colorism? Discuss your thought process around that.

9. Fellas, have you ever enabled colorism between Black women? In reviewing your relationship history, do you more or so date light-skin or dark-skinned Black women? Why?

10. Knowing the history behind colorism, what will you do, moving forward, to ensure that you do not perpetuate this destructive way of thinking?

—

Chapter 2: The Independent Black Woman- Unhealthy vs. Healthy

"Queen, you are smart, beautiful, funny, and definitely about your business. You are accomplished, honest, and you have morals and values, which is rare. When I think about the type of woman I would want to be with, I think about you. But you are a lot! Not in a bad way though; I just mean it takes a lot of work to be with a woman like you. You are very strong, independent and to be honest, you can be very intimidating. You don't play that shit! When a man steps to you, he got to come correct. A lot of men don't know how to approach a woman like you; and if they do manage to get through, they can't maintain or don't want to do the work. Instead of coming up to your level, they bring you down to theirs. Now, I'm not saying you should allow this; you absolutely shouldn't settle. You deserve the best! I'm just trying to help you understand the type of men that are out here."

This is a response from one of my male friends after yet another failed attempt at dating. Hearing this, I wasn't sure if I should feel special and complimented, or feel straight up defeated. Complimented, knowing that I have a lot of amazing qualities necessary for a healthy relationship, but defeated hearing that a lot of men aren't willing to "do the work," and they see me as "too much." So, I have one question…what is too much or a lot?

Is it the passion, strength, or directness? Or the confidence, intelligence, or encouragement? Or is it all of it? What is so wrong with a Black woman being passionate, strong, and direct? Or confident, intelligent, and encouraging? How can these qualities, when on their own, be so positive and #goals, but once a Black woman is added to the mix, we somehow transition these words into something negative? Instead of confidence, it's controlling, instead of direct, it's abrasive, and instead of encouragement, it's emasculation.

According to my friend, I am an independent Black woman, which ironically makes me non-preferred, even though I have many amazing qualities that also make me desirable. Are you just as confused as I am? If so, let's explore what it means to be an independent woman versus an independent Black woman.

"Hey Google. Define independent." Independent is not depending on another for livelihood (making a living).

"Hey Google. Define strong independent woman." Being a strong, independent woman means that you are able to find happiness on your own. You have self-confidence without having to rely on another person or society for validation. It means you have emotional independence and you're able to have healthy relationships with others without falling into co-dependent patterns.

"Hey Google. Describe an independent Black woman?" The independent Black woman is the depiction of a narcissistic, overachieving, and financially successful woman who emasculates the Black males in her life.

Wow! What a difference. You can clearly see how negative everything becomes by simply adding "Black" to the mix. Now, we can see why Black men are immediately turned off by the energy of strong independent "Black" women. They are perceiving the independent Black woman description versus the independent woman description.

Are there narcissistic, overachieving, and financially successful Black women who emasculates the Black males in their lives? Yes. But are there also Black women who are able to find happiness on their own, have self-confidence without having to rely on another person or society for validation, have emotional independence, and the ability to have healthy relationships with others without falling into co-dependent patterns? Yes.

Having the ability to distinguish between the unhealthy and healthy IBW is important when dating a Black woman. This distinction will not only help you learn to appreciate the Black woman even more, but it can also be the driving force behind the rebuilding of the Black family.

Based on the feedback I received, I have established four characteristic traits that make an IBW either unhealthy or healthy. With each characteristic trait, I have provided a brief detailed description. Do not think the information presented in this chapter is the end all be all of characteristic traits, or that these traits are only presented by women. The traits mentioned here were the ones most reported during the data collection process.

The Unhealthy-IBW

Most men are very familiar with the unhealthy IBW. This is the woman that America intended to create; she perpetuates the constructed mindset we have been plagued with. According to the feedback I received from Black men, she carries herself like she doesn't need a man financially, morally, and even physically. She out earns her male counterpart, and has confused financial freedom with being independent. Therefore, the lead in the home is determined by the money instead of the man.

Characteristics Traits

1. *Controlling- Expecting, compelling, or requiring others to cater to their own needs; even at another's expense.*

Since she out earns most Black men, this will determine his position in the household. Normally, a traditional man is the head of the home; the protector and the provider. In her mind, because the man is not the breadwinner, he should be in control, and therefore cannot be the head of the household.

She tends to tell a man what she thinks he should do, what he should wear, and how he should think. If there is a disagreement between them, she has a tendency of holding a grudge since she believes her way is the best way. She may be embarrassed by his occupation and if she does not approve of what his dreams are, she will not be supportive.

She may be very clingy. She will want to know who, what, when, where, why, and how; and if she cannot get in contact with him, she will call his phone and whoever else's phone until she is able to get in contact.

She may also be overly critical and judgmental; constantly pointing out what she sees as flaws and telling him what he needs to do to be better. No matter how much he improves, nothing will ever be good enough. He will be left feeling empty and doubting himself.

2. *Insensitive- Having a lack of care or concern for the feelings of others*

Due to her being overly concerned with her own needs, wants, and feelings, she will have a lack of regard for how she makes him feel. If she gives him advice and he doesn't follow it, this will upset her. She will not have emotion regulation and will resort to fighting unfair.

She will use strategies during conflicts to put the man on edge and force him to become defensive. She will yell and hit below the belt, bringing up past mistakes or unrelated issues to deflect or distract him from the actual issue. She will also bring up his known insecurities or past traumas, using it as ammunition to hurt him. Her ultimate goal is to be right, not to resolve.

3. *Emasculating- Depriving a man of his male role or identity.*

As a result of her belief that her financial success makes her superior in the relationship, she will use this ideology to make him feel less of a man. She may make statements like "I am the man of the house," "I wear the pants in this relationship," "I don't need no man," or I can take care of myself, if you don't like it then leave."

If she has children with him, she may undermine him in front of them; indirectly encouraging them to also disregard and disrespect him and his authority. When communicating with him, in private or in the company of others, she may yell at him and over him, not allowing him to speak. More than often, she may speak ill of him in front of other people, his children and/or on social media.

She will also withhold sex or intimacy; and in the midst of a conflict, she may make fun of him sexually. She may even make comparisons between him and her previous partners, both sexually and in general. She will also withhold any form of love, admiration, or appreciation, but constantly point out his flaws or lack of income. She may even refuse to speak to him; going long periods of time without speaking to him or acknowledging his presence. She will completely disregard him as a man and an overall human being.

4. *Unapologetic- Not acknowledging or expressing regret.*

This type of IBW may present everything previously mentioned, and do so unapologetically. She will not apologize, but instead deflect, make excuses and blame him in the process. She will be completely unbothered by the hurt she is causing. Not only will she be unbothered, but she may even find enjoyment in the process, displaying a harsh level of vindictiveness. Because there is no apology, there is also no changed behavior.

The Healthy-IBW

As I previously mentioned, most men are very familiar with the unhealthy IBW. Unfortunately, these men have either not had the pleasure of experiencing a healthy IBW, or weren't able to recognize her character traits. According to the feedback I received from Black men that are familiar with her, she handles her business, knows her worth, and contributes to the building of her family with her man. She 100% understands the importance of and values the Black man, and will gladly submit to his authentic masculinity.

Characteristics Traits

1. Confident-Ability to trust in oneself, trust in someone else and/or trust in something.

The healthy IBW is self-sufficient, accountable, and intellectually empowered. She may out earn a lot of Black men, but she does not allow finances to determine his position in her life or the home. She is more concerned with his morals, values, character, mindset, and her ability to trust him as a man. She may exude anger at times, but this does not come from being bitter. Instead, it usually comes from being the most disrespected and unprotected woman in this country. She carries herself with a great deal of self-respect and conviction, and is OK with being single. She will never feel the need to objectify herself for attention. She is very secure with who she is; showing trust in her man and earning his trust in return.

The world may view her as an alpha female, but she is actually an alpha submissive. She controls every aspect of her life; others may feel she wants to do the same with a man, but in reality, she craves the presence of a true alpha male that she can submit to and be protected by. Her goal is to feel 100% confident that she is safe in every aspect of the relationship, and in return she will devote herself to him mentally, emotionally and physically.

2. *Emotionally Intelligent- The ability to understand, use, and manage your own emotions in positive ways.*

Emotional intelligence is, by far, the most important of her characteristic traits. She is able to manage and relieve daily stressors in healthy ways, as well as control impulsive feelings and behaviors in order to prevent from saying or doing something negative towards the man in her life. If she happens to create a stressful situation for him, she will notice the signs and immediately stop whatever she is doing that is causing him stress. She wants to create and maintain a low stress environment.

She is very self-aware and is able to identify and express what she is feeling and why she feels that way. "I feel like _____ when you say/do _____." When she needs to bring something to his attention, she handles the situation with care so he doesn't feel attacked or torn down. She is driven by empathy and the desire to solve problems. Her goal is team work; to promote a healthy environment where him and her can both learn from each other and grow together.

3. Encouraging- Giving someone support and hope for future success.

As a result of her being emotionally intelligent, she welcomes change. She understands that change means growth. Since this is a part of her philosophy, she will ask about his wants and desires and then encourage him to go for them. Not only will she encourage him, but she will also actively participate in a way that's most helpful to his growth and wellbeing.

Although she is super supportive, she is not an enabler. When he appears to be going astray, she will hold him accountable and guide him back to the right path. Her goal is to encourage him to be the best version of himself in order for him to encourage her to be the best version of herself.

4. Apologetic- Regretfully acknowledging an offense or failure.

Since she thrives off emotional intelligence, this makes her very apologetic. Once she is aware of her wrong doings or mistakes, she will take accountability and actively work on preventing them from happening again. She finds zero pleasure in causing any hurt or distress towards her man. In fact, it pains her to know that he is hurt by something she has said or done and she will want to repair the damage immediately.

Understanding the differences between the mentality, behaviors, verbiage, and intentions of the unhealthy and healthy IBW is crucial. It can literally mean the difference between a relationship full of chaos and toxicity versus a relationship that is complete with overall safety and stability.

<u>Processing Session</u>

1. How do you feel about categorizing the IBW into healthy and unhealthy categories?

2. Ladies, which category do you fall into? How does it make you feel?

3. If you fall into the unhealthy category, what will you do to address the unhealthiness and evolve?

4. If you fall into the healthy category, will you support women with unhealthy characteristic traits? How will you do this?

5. Fellas, does understanding the difference between a healthy and unhealthy IBW change your perspective?

6. Based on this understanding, have there been unhealthy IBW you have stayed with, but shouldn't have?

7. Based on this understanding, have there been healthy IBW you should have stayed with, but didn't?

8. What were the reasons behind you either staying with an unhealthy IBW or leaving the healthy IBW? Moving forward, what will you do differently?

Part II: The Black Man

Dear Black Man

Dear Black Man
There is No-One like you

No-one as strong
No-one as **Powerful**
No-one more feared
Then the spirit inside of you

Racism is alive and ready
With you as the #1 target
Taking you out One by One
Without thinking twice about it

Although
They are willing to target any Black man
The **conscious** one is the one they really can't stand

The one who knows his history
The one who knows his rights
The one who takes his wealth of **knowledge** and uses it to **fight**

The one who stands his ground
And also takes a knee
The one who respects and **protects** the Black woman
The heart of the community

The one who understands
He is **indigenous** to this land
And the one who needs to "go back to where he came from"
Is the racist white man

BLACK MEN
Where are you?
We need you now more than ever
The time has come
For us to band our asses together

The **union** of the Black man and the Black woman
Is a force to be reckoned with
Any other union besides this is considered an offense

To Our culture, Our education
Our money, Our land

Our communities, Our **MINDS**
All the reasons we're hunted

BLACK ~~MEN~~
You are our leaders
Now stand up and **LEAD**

The essence of your presence
Will cause these racists to take heed

Show them
You will no longer be infected, threatened
Or ruled by oppression

Instead
You're going to stand strong
As a **collective**
With the Black Woman by your side
Holding her favorite fucking weapon

Queen X
7/4/2019

Chapter 3: War on the Black Man

Although the removal of the Black man is a strategy that has been used over the course of hundreds of years, it didn't stop the Black man and woman from marrying and maintaining strong Black family structures. Throughout slavery, the reconstruction era, and Jim Crow, Black men and women were still a representation of a strong unit. National data covering decennial years from 1890 to 1920 showed that Black people out-married white people, despite a consistent shortage of Black males. In 1965, only 25% of

Black families were headed by women. In 1983, that number more than doubled to 55%. So, what happened that triggered such a massive increase in the percentage?

According to Shahrazad Ali, "The Black woman's disrespect and rebellion against the leadership and authority of the Black man is the direct cause of the breakdown of the Black family." When Black women made the decision to join the women's liberation movement and accept the conditions of government assistance, that was when they decided to contribute to the destruction of the Black family.

Women's Liberation Movement

In 1920, the first wave of the feminist movement took place when the ratification of the 19th amendment gave women the right to vote. It's important to note that although it expanded voting rights to women, it did not address the racial terrorism that prevented Black people in the South from voting, regardless of sex. Prior to the 1965 Voting Rights Act, states blocked the Black vote by lying. They told Black people that their applications were incorrect or they had the wrong day and time. They also implemented poll tax, literacy tests, and had them recite the entire constitution.

The second wave of the feminist movement rode the coat tail of the Civil Rights Movement. In 1963, Betty Friedan published her book *The Feminine Mystique,* which contested the belief that a white woman's destiny was to get married and bear children. During this time, a white woman's path was one dedicated to homemaking; devoting her life to her husband and children. They were legally subjected to their husbands. They had no legal rights to any of his earnings or property, but their husbands had legal rights to theirs. The white woman's desire was to gain independence from the control of the white man.

Women occupied significant roles in organizations fighting for Civil Rights. The feminist leaders involved were inspired by the Civil rights movement through which they gained civic organizing experience. Being inspired, these women used this experience to form the organization NOW- National Organization for Women, which Black women joined. It was at this point that Black women turned their backs on Black men.

The Civil Rights Movement was about the Black man, Black woman, and Black child fighting for equality. The woman's liberation movement was about white women gaining independence from the control of white men. It made no sense for Black women to join this movement. According to Shahrazad Ali "We haven't been under the control of the Black man for over 500 years... what do we have to get liberated from?" This movement was not the Black woman's fight, and joining essentially put Black women against Black men.

Black women were fed the ideology of liberation by white women; being your own person, independent of the man. Since Black women were already conditioned psychologically to be in a state of independence, they were easily susceptible to this concept, even though it made absolutely no sense. What Black women didn't understand in joining this movement was that being independent of the Black man meant giving up their provider, their protection, and their parental coalition. It also meant leaving the Black woman to fend for herself, leaving the Black child without a stable family structure, and leaving the Black man without his purpose.

Welfare

Throughout the 1920s, the U.S economy expanded rapidly, and the nation's total wealth more than doubled between 1920 and 1929, a period dubbed "The Roaring Twenties." In 1929, the stock market crashed, causing the Great Depression. Families who had previously enjoyed economic security suddenly faced financial instability and, in some cases, ruin. By 1933, 15 million Americans were unemployed, accounting for 20% of the population.

In 1933, Franklin D Roosevelt was inaugurated, and within the first 100 days, he enacted what he called The New Deal. The New Deal was a collection of programs that were to provide immediate relief from the Great Depression and address reforms in industry, agriculture, finance, water, power, labor, and housing. These programs were meant to signal both an expansion of federal power and a transformation in the relationship between the federal government and the American people.

In 1935, the Social Security Act was established in order to protect families from loss of income. Level one provided income to the general population such as unemployment, retirement, and disability. Level two consisted of means-tested public assistance programs previously called Aid to Families with Dependent Children (AFDC), and is now called Temporary Assistance for Needy Families (TANF). Although this new safety net was seen to be a great economic resolve for the American people, it was problematic for a certain group of people during the decades of 1930 and 1940.

As mentioned earlier, level one of the SSA-1935 provided unemployment, retirement, and disability. These were considered work-related social insurance programs. These programs called for contributions through payroll taxes from both employers and employees. Due to racial discrimination in employment, Black people worked menial jobs and were paid off the books, making them ineligible for these social insurance programs.

During this time, Black people weren't able to benefit from AFDC either. The criteria for eligibility was determined by the state, so this barred them from full participation, because the country operated under "separate but equal." And we know it was anything but equal. Disadvantages for Black families furthered into the 1950s and 1960s, when States used different tactics to reduce enrollment and costs. Many tactics were used in order to prevent Black people from being eligible. Two factors in particular contributed to the breakdown of the Black family. They were the exclusion of poor families with two parents and the "Man in the house" rule.

Poor families with two parents were excluded from receiving AFDC using the 'able-bodied' argument (not physically disabled; strong and healthy). If one or both parents were able-bodied, then they didn't need AFDC because they were able to work and make a living; even though there was racial discrimination in employment against Black people. The "man in the house" rule allowed for midnight raids, and if the mother was caught with a man in the home, she would lose her benefits.

Under the "man in the house" rule, two situations were forbidden; (1) for a mother to reside with a man and child, whether he was the father or not, and (2) for a mother to have a relationship with a man, whether he was the father or not, even if he claimed to have a different residency.

Due to the use of these tactics, a lot of Black women chose to give up the Black man to receive AFDC.

In 1992, Bill Clinton promised to "end welfare as we know it." President Clinton submitted his revised welfare reform proposal to Congress in June 1996. On August 22, he signed the 1996 welfare reform bill that ended AFDC and replaced it with TANF.

Under federal law, families receiving TANF must sign their rights to child support payments over to the state, and is forced to sue the non-custodial parent (most likely the father). From the government's perspective, if you can provide economically, then you're a good father, and if you can't, then you're not.

Even if the father is unaware that the mother is receiving government assistance, they are still responsible for payments. Failure to pay child support is a federal offense and will result in several different penalties. The father can have his driver's license suspended, denial of passport, wages garnished, incur fines, and receive jail time. These penalties effect the Black man's ability to find a job, keep his job, travel on a daily basis, make a living for himself, enjoy his freedom, and most importantly, be a father.

Through child support, the mother is now the gatekeeper to whether or not the father can have a relationship with the child. For a lot of Black men, their ability to see their child is based on those child support payments. The system enforces the collection side of child support, but not access and visitation.

From 1970 to 1990, the two-parent Black family dropped, hitting 38%. As of 2019, less than 45% of Black children have a father in the home. The rate of Black out-of-wedlock births went from 24.5% in 1964 to 70.7% by 1994. Still to this day, over 70% of Black children are born without a father present in the home.

The breakdown of the Black family structure has the biggest impact on children. Family structure influences the choices that children make. Children without a father in the home are more likely to suffer from mental health problems as adults. Boys raised without their father are much more likely to use drugs, engage in violent or criminal behavior, drop out of school and go to jail. Girls are more likely to engage in early sexual activity or have a child out of wedlock.

According to Shahrazad Ali, "In the break-down of the relationship, each party shares 50% of the responsibility. So, for every child that's out there, out of control, disrespectful, ignorant, and uneducated, there is a Black mother who failed to do her job, and a Black father who failed to do his. To raise children, we need the parental coalition between the Black woman and the Black man. The Black man provides more in a Black home than financial support; he provides direction, guidance, gratification, and fulfillment for our children."

Mass Incarceration
Reagan

Although the breakdown of the Black family structure was directly impacted by Black women participating in the feminist movement and government assistance, mass incarceration was the icing on the cake. As mentioned earlier, mass incarceration is one of the biggest attacks on Black men. In 2018, Black people represented 33% of the sentenced prison population, nearly triple their 12% share of the U.S. adult population. So, how did this happen? How did Black people end up making up the largest population in prison, while simultaneously being the smallest percentage in the country?

Back in 1981, the New York Times published an article called Philadelphia Suffers in Manufacturing Job Exodus. Although the article was specifically discussing Philadelphia, it was actually a national phenomenon affecting many other old industrial cities. Between 1970 and 1980, manufacturing jobs had declined from 26% to 17%, falling by 140,000. Not only did Philadelphia lose its jobs, but it also lost its people.

According to a survey conducted, roughly 70% of the manufacturing jobs held were by people who actually lived in the city of Philadelphia, while only 30% of the office workers were city dwellers. The middle class and those desperately trying to improve themselves left, causing the population to drop from 1.85 million to 1.69 million. Those left behind were the people who couldn't afford to leave and couldn't afford to live.

During this same decade, all of the industrial building trade programs were removed from the inner-city high schools. Before the removal, young Black boys were able to graduate from a trade program, become licensed and ready to work. This was no longer an option. The removal of these programs, combined with the effects of deindustrialization, left Black youth with no way to make a living for themselves or their families.

After Ronald Reagan took office in 1981, he declared a war on drugs in 1982. It's quite ironic that when he enforced the war on drugs, the crack epidemic began in the Black community. Out of desperation, Black men began selling crack in their own neighborhoods, causing ruin and destruction; people strung out and the environment was toxic/unsafe. In 1985, the number of people who said they used cocaine on a regular basis increased from 4.2 million to 5.8 million. Emergency room visits for cocaine-related incidents increased between 1984 and 1987.

In 1986, Reagan signed the Anti-Drug Abuse Act. This law established more severe mandatory sentences for drug offenses. The typical mandatory minimum sentences for many drug crimes became 5-10 years, even for relatively low-level drug crimes. At the start of Reagan's term, the total prison population was 329,821. When he left office in 1989, the prison population had doubled to 627,588. The number of people incarcerated for nonviolent drug offenses increased from 50,000 in 1980 to 400,000 in 1997.

The strategic implementation of crack in the inner cities provided young Black men, who could not find a legal job, a way to make a living. By selling crack to feed themselves, Black men inadvertently fed themselves to the United States prison system via the war on drugs.

Hip-Hop

"In 1991, I was invited to a secret meeting with about 25 other people who worked in the music industry. Before anyone was informed about what the meeting was about, we were asked to sign confidentiality agreements and were informed that those in violation of this agreement would lose their jobs. Some refused and left, while others signed and stayed. In the meeting we were informed that the companies they worked for, had invested millions in the industry of privatized prisons and that our position of influence in the music industry would impact the profitability of these investments. It was further explained that these prisons will become publicly traded and they would be able to buy shares, but this would only work after receiving funding from the government based on the number of inmates; the more inmates, the more money. Still confused about what it had to do with the people in the room, it was added that it was now in their interest to make sure that these prisons

remained filled. Their job would be to help make this happen by marketing music that promotes criminal behavior, rap being the music of choice. Due to some being in complete disbelief, chaos erupted and a group, including myself, were escorted out. I was reminded when my industry colleague, who had opened the meeting earlier, hurried out to meet us and reminded us that we had signed an agreement and would suffer the consequences of speaking about this publicly, or even with those who attended the meeting. I asked him why he was involved with something this corrupt and he replied "that it was bigger than the music business and nothing we'd want to challenge without risking consequences." We all protested, and as he walked back into the house, I remember word for word the last thing he said, "It's out of my hands now."

This letter was written by an individual who was present at the meeting and decided to remain anonymous; fearing for his life and the life of his family. This letter reports that the music industry strategically promoted criminal behavior in rap music in order to condition the listener and encourage criminal behavior. This strategy was used to ensure that the prisons remained full and the owners remained rich. The mass majority of listeners of rap music are young Black boys in the hood, and the highest percentage of inmates are Black men. I guess it's true what they say; "Control the Music, Control the Children."

Clinton

"And those who commit repeated violent crimes should be told, when you commit a third violent crime, you will be put away for good; three strikes you're out."

-Bill Clinton 1994

As part of the US Justice Department Anti-Violence strategy of 1984, the Clinton administration released its version of "Three Strikes and you're out" crime measure. The three strikes law imposed longer prison sentences for certain repeat offenders, as well as instituted other changes. Most significantly, it required that a person who is convicted of a felony and who has been previously convicted of one or more violent, or serious felonies (drug crimes) receive a sentence enhancement. Under the three strikes law, a felon convicted of a federal crime for the third time would be sentenced to prison for life.

The three strikes law didn't allow leeway for judges, even for individuals with a minor criminal past. California had a particularly strict three strikes law passed in 1994, which the New York Times indicated had led to people facing life in prison for stealing work gloves or passing a bad check. Like mandatory minimum sentencing laws, the three strikes law meant that the only opportunity for defendants to protect their future is to avoid conviction.

According to Michelle Alexander, the war on drugs was a response to the Civil Rights movement, which undermined the white power structure of racial hierarchy. The incarceration of Black men was a way to get society back under white control. Black imprisonment is merely a changing of the rules so that white society can legally oppress Black men for political, social, and economic domination.

Processing Session

1. What are your thoughts on Black women joining the women's liberation movement? Did it make sense?

2. What are your thoughts surrounding mass incarceration via Hip-Hop and privatized prisons? Will this change your perspective of what type of music you listen to or share?

3. If you receive public assistance, what is your plan to move away from needing public assistance?

4. If you receive public assistance, have you ever used the rules of public assistance to be vindictive against a Black man? If yes, why? And what are you going to do to change this moving forward?

5. Why do child support payments determine whether a father can see his child/children?

6. Since we know that keeping a child away from their father can have adverse effects, how will you move forward with ensuring that children have a relationship with their father (with or without child support payments)?

7. Does understanding the war on Black men change your perspective on the current state of Black men in this country?

8. With this understanding, what will you do to ensure that you aren't contributing to the war on Black men moving forward?

Chapter 4: The Black Man Unhealthy vs. Healthy

In reviewing the feedback I received from Black men, I found it very interesting that 100% of them said "Yes. I am a good Black man," but about 50% admitted they were either unhealthy mentally and emotionally or said they were unsure. In the introduction, it was explained that there is a difference between a good person and a healthy person. It was highlighted that a good person can exist without being healthy, but a healthy person cannot exist without being good.

When trying to be the Black man in the life of a Black woman, having the ability to distinguish between those unhealthy and healthy characteristic traits are extremely important. If you can't identify the unhealthy in yourself then you won't be able to avoid the unhealthy in another; making you susceptible to toxic relationships.

The feedback I received allowed me to identify 5 characteristic traits that make a Black man either unhealthy or healthy. With each characteristic trait, I have provided a brief detailed description. As previously mentioned, do not think the information presented in this chapter is the end all be all of characteristic traits, or that these traits are only presented by men. The traits mentioned here were the ones most reported during the data collection process.

The Unhealthy-BM

The description of the unhealthy Black man is normally provided by Black women. I made it a point to ensure that when discussing the unhealthy BM, I quoted Black men only. According to Black men, the unhealthy BM has had years of victimization; without resolving any of the issues. He is not expressive with how he feels; instead, he holds everything in, which results in bad communication and blaming others for his mistakes. Due to years of being victimized, he struggles to feel in control. This can trigger him to be overly controlling or domineering within his relationship and household.

Characteristics Traits

1. *Provider/Leech-Earns a steady income which enables him to provide food, shelter, and materialistic things for his family or living off of the woman he is with while simultaneously draining her mentally and emotionally.*

It seems for unhealthy BM, money equals power. He will often use his position as the provider to dominate in the home and the relationship, "I make the money so I make the rules." An unhealthy BM will also neglect (sometimes unknowingly) other parts of the relationship and use being a provider as an excuse. "I work, I pay the bills, I put food on the table and buy things you need/want, and you still find something to complain about."

If he is a leech, he will prey on or cling to a woman like a human parasite. He will be financially draining to the woman he is with. He will either be the one at home all day or out with friends (possibly driving her car), lavishing her resources. Regardless if he is a financial provider or a leech, he will simultaneously be mentally and emotionally draining.

2. *Unsafe- Dangerous or likely to cause harm or damage.*

The more obvious signs of a lack of safety are physical and verbal abuse. Physical abuse is when he intentionally makes physical contact, using any part of his body or an object in private, or in public. It is still physical abuse with or without leaving bruises. Verbal abuse can be him calling her names like stupid, dumb, ugly, not good enough or weight shaming "Why can't you do what I want you to do, to be how I want you to be? You're going to force me to look for what I want somewhere else."

He may also yell at her, and demean her in private and in public to make himself "look and feel like a man." He may also justify the abuse by trying to minimize the verbal abuse; "At least I'm not beating and cheating," or "This is as good as you're going to get...no one else is going to love you better than I do."

Less obvious signs of a lack of safety can look like passive and aggressive manipulation. Passive manipulation can include a pattern of lies and sneaky behavior where he is intentionally deceptive in order to get his way. The goal is to get what he wants, by getting her to do something she doesn't want to do. This form of manipulation could include, but is not limited to, getting her to participate in a threesome, persuading her to invest money into something risky or changing something about her appearance.

A more aggressive form of manipulation would be a tactic called gaslighting. Gaslighting is a malicious method used by narcissists. It causes her to question her sanity and doubt her memories. This tactic is used in order to gain power and control; something like mental rape. Gaslighting will begin small, where he will make her think she misheard something he said, but as time goes on, it will progressively get worse. She will discuss detailed conversations with him and he will insist those conversations went completely different or it didn't happen at all. He may also create memories that didn't happen, causing her to doubt herself. In the end, he will drive her to feel like she is crazy.

3. *Impulsivity- Acting or doing something without forethought.*

An unhealthy BM will certainly display impulsive behaviors throughout the relationship. His impulsivity will present themselves during conflicts. He will never admit his weaknesses or faults, but instead, he will be very anxious to challenge things in order to avoid criticism. When something doesn't go the way he planned, he will respond by throwing a tantrum. When he needs to make an important life decision or is put in a stressful situation, he will fail to analyze the pros and cons. Instead, he will have bad judgment, ultimately make the situation worse.

4. *Vulnerable- Susceptible to physical or emotional attack or harm.*

Most people associate being vulnerable with being able to allow your partner to get to know all of you, and this is not only correct, but healthy. The type of vulnerability an unhealthy BM may have is the one that allows him to be "weakened." If he is presented with obstacles in life, he will most likely become defeated, and he will refuse to keep trying or change. He will make excuse after excuse as to why things don't work out in his favor. "Oh woe is me." He will be completely unmotivated and lack resilience. He will not learn from life, but instead, be consumed by it.

5. *Unapologetic- Not acknowledging or expressing regret.*

The unhealthy BM will present all of the previously mentioned, and do so unapologetically. Just like the unhealthy BW, he will not apologize, but instead become defensive, deflect, make excuses, and never take accountability. Most times, he will be completely unbothered by the hurt his attitude is causing to his partner. Not only will he be unbothered, but at times, hurting her will simultaneously make him feel like a man. If he does happen to be "bothered" by the hurt he caused, he will justify why it was necessary "Man, you see what you did. I don't mean to make you feel like this, but you be doing too much. You don't listen." Similar to the unhealthy BW, because there will be no apology, there will also be no changed behavior.

The Healthy-BM

The data I received from Black men showed that they seem to have a unanimous description of the characteristic traits of a healthy BM. It appears that a healthy BM is very level headed and operates from a place of low stress. He is honorable in all aspects of his life (friend, father, partner, etc.) and he is also a provider. He doesn't just provide financially, but in any other way his support is needed. Self-care is necessary for him to maintain a balance between being an individual and being the head of the household.

Characteristics Traits

1. *Provider- Earns a steady income which enables him to provide food, shelter, and <u>daily necessities</u> for his family.*

The healthy BM is the Black man white supremacy wants to destroy. He is the man that ensures that his family is taken care of financially, but financial stability is not all he provides. He also provides spiritual guidance and leadership (whatever that looks like for him and his family). He finds an educational moment in every part of life, in order to teach and raise strong and resilient descendants. He provides emotional support and safety, allowing his woman to feel emotionally safe and secure with being her true self, while teaching his children the same. Lastly, he provides overall protection for his family, especially the Black woman.

2. Safe-Protecting from or unlikely to cause danger, risk, or injury.

The healthy BM is a man who secures the physical, mental, and emotional safety of his woman. He will make it a point to make sure she feels protected. He will not allow anyone to disrespect or degrade her at any time. He will also encourage her to feel comfortable being herself and expressing how she feels. His goal is to build a healthy relationship fostered by trust and honesty. Above all, he is a man of his word.

3. Emotional Intelligence- The ability to understand, use, and manage your own emotions in positive ways

Just as it was explained for the healthy BW, emotional intelligence is also one of the most important of his characteristic traits. The Black man has it extremely hard on a daily basis and this skill allows him to manage those daily stressors in healthy ways. The healthy BM will not act on impulse, rather he will express how he is feeling, why he feels that way, and what he needs to make himself feel better about things. He is driven by compassion and will make sure his woman's concerns are not only heard, but resolved. He will

not want to go to bed angry. His goal is to promote a stress-free environment where they both
can feel loved and appreciated.

4. *Resilience- The ability to recover quickly from dif-
ficulties and become healthy again.*

Since the healthy BM is the one white supremacy wants to destroy, resilience is important.
This allows him to utilize different methods of
self-care in order to recover from adversities. He
will not be weakened by the many different attacks made on him on a daily basis. He will learn
and grow from life instead of being consumed by
it.

5. *Apologetic- Regretfully acknowledging an offense
or failure.*

Since he operates from a place of low stress
and compassion, this makes him apologetic. Once
he is aware that something he said or did has
caused his woman hurt, he will want to do what
is necessary to maintain that low-stress environment. He will listen to her concerns, take accountability when necessary, and effectively apologize to keep the relationship moving forward.

As a Black man, understanding whether you
are unhealthy or healthy is crucial before deciding

to be the man in the life of a healthy BW. Remember, if you can't identify the unhealthy in yourself, then you won't be able to avoid the unhealthy in another; making you susceptible to toxic relationships. Your presence alone can cause either a positive or negative shift in the relationship. Therefore, if you are unhealthy, you will cause complete chaos. But if you are healthy, you will be a complete blessing.

Processing Session

1. How do you feel about categorizing the BM into unhealthy and healthy categories?
2. Ladies, does understanding the difference between an unhealthy and healthy BM change your perspective?
3. Fellas, which category do you fall into? How does it make you feel?
4. If you fall into the unhealthy category, what will you do to address the unhealthiness and evolve?
5. If you fall into the healthy category, will you support other men with unhealthy characteristic traits? How will you do this?

6. Ladies, based on this understanding, have there been unhealthy BM you have stayed with, but shouldn't have?

7. Based on this understanding, have there been healthy BM you should have stayed with, but didn't?

8. What were the reasons behind you either staying with an unhealthy BM or leaving the healthy BM? Moving Forward, what will you do differently?

Part III: Relationship
Tug of War

Tug of War

You say
"Let's promise to always have
great communication" and we
agree
But loud, criticizing or avoiding
Is how you choose to be

Anger, frustration, and annoy-
ance
You are entitled to feel
But how you choose to show
these emotions
Is simply unreal

When you're challenged or con-
fronted
The blame is on me
You deflect and disrespect
And it never ends with a real
apology

A person can fail many times
When working on improving
themselves
But a person only becomes a
failure
When they blame someone else

Tug of War is a game we con-
stantly seem to play
I pull you up
You pull me down
I encourage you forward
You jerk me around

I tell you what I need
To feel emotionally safe and secure
But you think I'm being controlling
Because you're too damn emotionally immature

Communication is the key
To having a successful relation-
ship
It's the beginning of a strong
foundation
And it should not be skipped

We've been going back and
forth for a while now
And it seems all I've done is
wait

Wait for you to try
Wait for your trust
Wait for your respect

Wait for you to emotionally
evolve
Wait for an apology
Wait for you to change your
mindset

Now, here we are
You refuse to accept responsi-
bility and change
So I guess this is the end
Because I'm done with this
toxic exchange

QueenX
9/12/2015

Chapter 5: Unhealthy Black Men and Healthy Black Women

This next section will be dedicated to focusing on the relationship between unhealthy BM and healthy BW. This section will highlight why there is so much of a tug of war/conflict between the two. To begin, here is an analogy I will use to explain the healthy BW and her experiences with unhealthy BM. Since men cherish their cars, I will be using the "driving a car" analogy. The car will be an analogy for her life and driving will be an analogy for having control over the journey.

On her journey, she is driving and has full control over where she goes, how she gets there, and what happens along the way (outside of things she cannot control). Examples include, but are not limited to, switching lanes or getting off on an exit by signaling and driving safely. Not allowing her gas tank to get below half a tank, and having maintenance done accordingly. Using her GPS or stopping to ask for directions if she gets lost, and determining who gets in the car to take the journey with her.

On her journey, she will encounter 3 out of 4 types of men. The first type of man she will encounter is the one she will not even allow in her car. This man is clearly unhealthy and is likely to keep her from getting to her destination, and will probably cause an accident in the process.

The second type of man she will encounter is the one who she lets get in the car, but never allows him to drive. This man appears to be a good man to journey with, but after letting him in, she sees that he has a bit of road rage and doesn't make her feel comfortable enough to let him drive her car. She inevitably leaves him at a truck stop.

The third type of guy she will encounter is the one she runs into the most. This man leads her to believe he can drive and he actually gets her to let him drive her car. Unfortunately, while driving, she realizes that he is not equipped to be driving her car. For some reason, he starts speeding, recklessly switching lanes with no turn signal, he misses the exit, refuses to ask for directions, ignores the low oil warning light, and damn near ran out of gas. And what is she doing during all of this?

She is pointing out that he is driving too fast and reckless, he isn't signaling, he missed the exit, the car is low on gas, and he needs to get the car serviced for an oil change. And how does he respond to her? "See that's the problem with ya'll women. Ya'll don't know how to let a man be a man! Always trying to control everything and tell us what to do. Don't no man want no controlling ass woman. We not tryna hear all that."

Correction. This woman is not trying to control him or tell him what to do. She was led to believe that he, not only knew how to drive, but always took precautions before, during, and after driving. She is simply trying to get to her destination without getting a ticket, being stuck on the side of the road, or getting into an accident. Unfortunately, because he is unhealthy, he cannot distinguish between her and a back-seat driver.

A tug of war between the unhealthy BM and the healthy BW is inevitable. There is nothing more emotionally exhausting for a healthy BW than trying to unconditionally love a man that doesn't know how to be loved and doesn't know how to love in return. No matter what she says or does, it seems like her efforts fall on deaf ears and blind eyes.

In order to understand the cause behind the tug of war, I received feedback from Black men who disclosed they have experienced a healthy BW but ruined the relationship. After reviewing the data, I noticed a pattern in these five areas; communication, intimidation (financially/intellectually), emotional unsafety, fighting unfair, and apologies. Let's review each area to get a better depiction of how these areas lead to a tug of war.

Problem Areas

1. Communication

Communication allows someone to explain to another what they are experiencing, why they are experiencing it, and what their needs are.

Communication also allows for someone to listen, comprehend, and respond appropriately to what they hear. Sadly, when a healthy BW is in a relationship with an unhealthy BM, this exchange does not exist. Instead, when she brings something to his attention, regardless of how simple it may seem to her, he reacts irrationally.

When she is trying to teach him what she needs to feel loved, he will interpret this as trying to control him. When she holds him accountable for something, he will interpret this as nagging. When he hears that something he said or did made her feel hurt, or uncomfortable, he interprets this as he cannot do anything right and she is never happy.

These reactions, although irrational, are quite authentic and automatic. He may feel like he is under attack, being judged, being controlled, or believe it or not, severely overwhelmed, and anxious. These feelings result in him becoming defensive, disrespectful, and/or distant, refusing to even address the issue at all.

2. Intimidation (Financially/Intellectually)

It appears as though a lot of unhealthy BM are not 100% comfortable with the healthy BW being more successful and making more money.

It was confirmed that she never brings it up or throws it in their face. It's the simple fact that a man is supposed to be the provider, and how can he be the provider if the woman is the breadwinner? Remember, for an unhealthy BM, money equals power. So, if the woman has the money, then she also has the power; and that perceived power is viewed as an attack on their manhood.

Another part to this is the concept of intelligence. It seems that a Black woman making more money is not the only problem, but her intellect as well. Since Black women are outpacing Black men in higher education, there is a perception that they are also more intelligent. So, the unhealthy BM feels intimidated by her intelligence because he feels as though he can't "keep up." This internal struggle leads him to feel insecure, and eventually his discomfort will reveal itself in defensive behaviors such as being verbally combative or overcompensation (everything BIG).

3. Emotional Unsafety

Emotional safety is achieved in relationships where each individual is open and vulnerable, preventing the need to be defensive. They feel free to let down their guard and show their authentic self, including hurts, fears, and longings.

In order for the Black man and woman to have a healthy relationship, there must be emotional safety.

When dating an unhealthy BM, the Black woman is at risk of being put in a very emotionally unsafe situation. Since she is healthy, she is most likely to let her guard down and allow herself to be vulnerable. Unfortunately, because he is not healthy, he won't return the same level of vulnerability. Instead, he will think something like "This is too good to be true, something must be wrong," "She is out to get me. I have to get her before she gets me," "It's not safe. I need to maintain control."

These thoughts will activate his stress response system, which leads to him fighting unfair. He will start to disconnect from her emotionally, stonewalling, communicating through text only, becoming extremely defensive, and may even leave the relationship abruptly without notice. In the end, she will be more worried about how he will respond to what she needs to say, instead of focusing on what she needs to talk to him about. It will feel like fighting for him and the relationship alone, while walking on egg shells at the same time; thereby creating an emotionally unsafety situation.

4. Fighting Unfair

Fighting unfair involves using a strategy that doesn't serve to help bring understanding or resolve the conflict. Examples include stonewalling, communicating through text only, character assassination, invalidation, all or nothing phrases, and/or abrupt decisions in the midst of the conflict. When an unhealthy BM is dating a healthy BW, it can be guaranteed that he will utilize the majority of these strategies.

When an unhealthy BM stonewalls, he will hang up abruptly and refuse to answer the phone. In most cases, if he does respond, he will only text. When physically present, the moment he hears something he doesn't like, he will walk away or shut down, completely refusing to respond. During the conflict, he will invalidate her feelings by saying she shouldn't feel that way or deny making her feel that way at all. He may also label her as overly emotional and unstable, and himself as rational.

When he uses character assassination, he chooses to bring up the past. *"You stayed with your ex after he cheated with your best friend…how confident were you then?"* Or unrelated issues like *"At least I didn't stand you up on your birthday like he did"* to deflect from the actual issue. When trying to prove a point, instead of providing specific examples, he will use all or nothing phrases. He will tell her she is always nagging and complaining or she is never satisfied and will never be happy.

The goal of using these strategies is to be right, not to resolve. These strategies are completely counter-productive, and will definitely cause an escalation in the argument that will trigger his stress response. Once he is in fight or flight, he may become so overwhelmed, frustrated, or angry that he might make a decision that he may end up regretting; like cheating or ending the relationship altogether.

5. *Apologies*

Black men, have you ever said sorry and felt like it wasn't good enough? Black women, has a man ever said "I said I was sorry. I might not have said it how you wanted me to say it, but I did say it?" Based on the feedback I received from Black men, the answer to both of these questions is "yes." It was also confirmed that this leads to a huge tug of war. How can there be a resolution when there isn't an apology? Or when there is one, it isn't accepted?

Believe it or not, there is such a thing as an apology language. Although I am speaking about all healthy BW, the apology language needed will depend on the specific Black woman he is with. Unfortunately, the unhealthy BM will not use this information to learn how to effectively apologize and maintain a healthy relationship. Instead, he will interpret this as nothing is good enough for her, and/or she is trying to control how he speaks and wants everything done her way. Ultimately, these thoughts will prevent him from seeing the benefit in effective apologies.

Let's revisit the "driving a car" analogy from earlier. It would benefit unhealthy BM to understand that when they get into the car of healthy BW (enter her life), she has been the one in complete control. When she allows him to drive her car (take lead in her life and home), she is relinquishing a lot of control with the expectation that he will do what's needed to prevent a break down or accident (broken heart and unnecessary life/relationship struggles). When he begins driving recklessly; not taking any direction and neglecting the car (causing tug of wars and disregarding the life/relationship she is trying to nurture with him), he causes chaos and damage, figuratively and literally.

It's understood when an unhealthy BM says "I'm not perfect" in response to the needs of a healthy BW. She doesn't want him to be perfect, she wants him to be healthy. A perfect relationship would be one without conflict (which doesn't exist). A healthy relationship is one with conflict. Conflicts are inevitable in a relationship, but a healthy approach can make it easier to deal with those conflicts, and help build a stronger and healthier connection. This thing called a relationship is not easy, but it doesn't have to result in constant distress either.

Processing Session

Unhealthy Black Men

1. Does the driving a car analogy help change your perspective and understanding of a healthy BW?

2. Do you agree or disagree with the problem areas for the unhealthy BM in relationships with healthy BW? Discuss it?

3. Which problem areas would you say you participated in the most in your relationships?

4. Now that you are clear on the problems unhealthy BM create in relationships with healthy BW, what will you do to address these problematic behaviors and evolve into a healthy BM?

Healthy Black Women

1. Do you think the driving a car analogy puts a healthy BW's experience with an unhealthy man into its proper perspective? Why or Why not?

2. Which problem areas would you say you experienced the most in your relationships with unhealthy BM? Which one was the worst to encounter?

3. How did you address these problem areas?

4. How has dating an unhealthy BM affected your mindset around relationships/marriage?

Chapter 6: Unhealthy Black Women and Healthy Black Men

Since the conflicts that take place between unhealthy BM and the healthy BW were discussed, it's only right that the conflicts that take place between the healthy BM and the unhealthy BW are also discussed. Too often Black women are quick to tell a Black man all the things he is doing wrong or what he can do better, but not often do we hold Black women accountable for their behaviors towards men. To begin, I will be using the same "driving a car" analogy as before, but this time it will be from the perspective of a healthy BM.

Just like the healthy BW, the healthy BM is also driving and has full control over where he goes, how he gets there, and what happens along the way (outside of things he cannot control). On his journey, he will also encounter 3 out of 4 types of women. The first type of woman he will encounter is the one he will not allow in his car. This woman presents herself as loud, disrespectful, and "ratchet." She is likely to be a complete distraction, causing a stress induced accident in the process.

The second type of woman he will encounter is the one who he lets get in the car, but her presence doesn't last long. She is very attractive and appears to be a good woman to journey with, but after letting her in, she presents some concerning behaviors. He notices that she is overly emotional and thoughtless. This doesn't make him feel relaxed and secure enough to drive with her in the car and he eventually drops her off at the bus stop.

The third type of woman he will encounter, is the one that he will run into the most. She is also beautiful, smart, funny, and got her life in order. She leads him to believe that she is appreciative of a man who can drive, and that she understands her role on the journey. Unfortunately, while driving, he realizes that it was not productive to journey with this woman either. After some time, she begins backseat driving.

"Why or why aren't you driving the speed limit? Why did you get an oil change there, when I told you to go here? Why did you go this way instead of the other way? Who taught you how to drive? You need to take my directions because you know you don't know where you're going. If you had gone the way I told you to go, we wouldn't have gotten a flat tire. Do you even know how to fix a flat tire? I'm going to ask someone for help because I don't think you know what you are doing?"

Contrary to the healthy BW, this woman is trying to control him and tell him what to do. He is simply trying to get to his destination in the safest and least stressful way possible. Unfortunately, because she is unhealthy, she doesn't have the ability to identify and appreciate the healthy BM. She will not allow him to drive in peace and be of support when he needs it.

In order to understand the cause behind the tug of war, I received feedback from Black men who consider themselves healthy and have been in relationships with unhealthy BW. After reviewing the information, I was shocked at how similar the responses were. I was easily able to identify 5 areas that cause conflict in this relationship; communication, controlling, neglect, insecurities, and apologies. Let's review each one to get a better depiction of how these areas lead to a tug of war.

Problem Areas

1. Communication

As explained earlier, communication allows someone to explain to another what they are experiencing, why they are experiencing it, and what their needs are. Sadly, when a healthy BM is in a relationship with an unhealthy BW, this does not exist. Instead, when she feels the need to communicate with him, she uses unfair tactics, which results in different forms of emasculation.

Since he is a healthy BM, he will allow her to get to know all of him. Since she is unhealthy, she will use things that she has learned as ammunition during conflicts. In the midst of conflicts, he may hear something like "Maybe if your mother treated you better, you would know how to treat me" or "Who you think you talking to? You must be smoking crack again."

When communicating with him, whether in private or in the company of others (kids included), she will yell, talk at him, and over him, not allowing him to speak. She will also be overly critical and harsh with verbal attacks. She may speak on how he makes a living, point out what she sees as flaws and mistakes, or highlight his sexual shortcomings. She completely disrespects him as a man and human being.

2. Controlling

If she makes equivalent or more money than him, this will lead her to feel superior in the relationship. He will probably hear her say things like "I don't need you or no man. If you don't like it, you can leave" or "You can tell me what to do when you can afford to tell me what to do."

She will operate from a "my way is the right way" mindset, and expects him to follow suit. If he doesn't, she will respond with an attitude; leading to an unnecessary conflict. She will have a tendency of holding a grudge, which will result in emasculation by her withholding sex or intimacy. There will be a complete battle for "control" because she will not submit to the idea that being the head of the home is his rightful position.

3. Insecurities

When reviewing the data, trust issues in unhealthy BW was overwhelmingly reported by both unhealthy and healthy BM. It was reported that she will be very possessive, wanting to tag along everywhere he goes. She will also be very accusatory. "Why she looking at you like that, what y'all know each other?" or "Why don't you want me to go, what you going to go see another girl?" As stated in a chapter two, she will be very clingy. She will want to know who, what, when, where, why, and how; and if she cannot get in contact with him, she will call his phone and whoever else's phone until she is able to make contact. If she is unable to contact him by phone, she will have no problem doing a "pop-up."

4. Neglectful

Just like trust issues, neglect by unhealthy BW was also overwhelmingly reported by both unhealthy and healthy BM. This feedback was especially hard to read about and listen to because it depicts the love and support Black men crave from Black women, but aren't receiving. It was clear that they want to be comfortable with making themselves emotionally vulnerable to a woman, but they fear emotional rejection (the feeling a person experiences when disappointed about not achieving something desired). It was reported that the mistreatment from the unhealthy BW leaves healthy BM with hurt feelings; hurt he can't express because she will not care.

She will withhold any form of admiration or appreciation for what he is doing right, but constantly point out his flaws and what she believes he could do better. When an unhealthy BW is "in a mood," all the love she claims she has for him disappears. Whatever love she gives comes with conditions. There is no such thing as unconditional love with an unhealthy BW.

5. *Apologies*

Black women, have you ever said to a Black man "I apologize? Black men, have you ever heard a Black woman say, "I apologize"? According to the feedback I received from Black men, the answer to both of these questions is "no." How can there be a resolution when there isn't an apology, or when the woman always expects the man to apologize, but she never does.

The unhealthy BW may present all of the previously mentioned, and she will do so unapologetically. Since she operates from a "my way is the right way" mindset, she will see no fault in what she says or does in the relationship. Instead, she will blame him for all their problems. As explained earlier, she will be completely unbothered by the hurt she is causing him. Not only will she be unbothered, but she may even find enjoyment in the process, displaying a harsh level of vindictiveness.

Let's revisit the "driving a car" analogy from earlier. It would benefit unhealthy BW to understand that when they get into the car of healthy BM (enter his life), being in control is his rightful position. When she allows him to drive in peace (be a source of support and encouragement), yes, she is relinquishing a lot of control, but she will be safe and he will do everything required to get them to their destination (protect and provide for her and his family while building a life). When she starts backseat driving (causing a tug of war and creating a stressful environment), she causes destruction, figuratively and literally.

Processing Session

Unhealthy Black Women

1. Does the driving a car analogy help change your perspective of and understand healthy BM?

2. Do you agree or disagree with the problem areas for the unhealthy BW in relationships with healthy BM? Discuss it?

3. Which problem areas would you say you participated in the most in your relationships?

4. Now that you are clear on the problems unhealthy BW create in relationships with healthy BM, what will you do to address these problematic behaviors and evolve into a healthy BW?

Healthy Black Men

1. Do you think the driving a car analogy puts a healthy BM's experience with an unhealthy woman into its proper perspective? Why or Why not?

2. Which problem areas would you say you experienced the most in your relationships

with unhealthy BW? Which one was the worst to encounter?

3. How did you address these problem areas?
4. How has dating an unhealthy BW affected your mindset around relationships/marriage?

Part IV: Trauma

Emotions

Hurt, Anger, Pain
Oh how these emotions
Can drive a person insane

Drained-of
All of your energy
and serenity
Trying to maintain

A relationship with someone
You admire, desire
But has left you feeling
Defamed…Shamed…

How do you sustain?

Worry, Fear, Anxiety
Oh how these emotions
Can cripple you entirely

Creating an unhealthy
disassociation from society
In spite of thee
Encouragement and
Nourishment
Provided by me

You Suffer…

Silently

Devalued, Humiliated,
Dismissed
Oh how these emotions
Can leave you feeling pissed

After someone insisted
You belong and seals it
With a kiss, then
Inadvertently makes you feel
like
You never existed

Not realizing
They're creating problems
Due to Traumas that
pre-existed

Damn.
How did I get tricked?
QueenX
1/30/2019

Chapter 7: What is Trauma?

Human beings are naturally social beings. From the time we are born, everything about our development is shaped by our social interactions. The most significant of these interactions typically happens in early childhood, between the ages of 0-5. This is the time where we form our first attachment with others, particularly our caregivers. This secure attachment creates a solid foundation for understanding yourself and others. The reason a secure attachment is so important is because attachment is the emotional bond that is formed in order to establish a sense of safety and security. For children to experience a healthy development, they must be born and raised in an environment that provides safety/protection, comfort, and consistency via a secure attachment. Trauma can derail this development without the presence of a secure attachment.

For example, let's say two trains leave Philadelphia headed for California. In the midst of the journey, an unforeseen accident takes place, damaging both trains and knocking them off track. So now, both trains are damaged and not headed in the correct direction. Train A has a conductor that pulls the train into the next available train station to fix the damages and get the train back on track to California. Now, train A can continue the journey, picking up/dropping off the passengers as planned, and making it to its intended destination.

Train B has a conductor, but this conductor neglects fixing the damages and getting the train back on track. Instead, the conductor continues on that same path, not knowing where it's going. Train B starts dropping people off in the wrong places and picking up the wrong people along the way. Train B is also receiving more damages either from the passengers or from the route itself. Train B not only never makes it to the intended destination, but ends up in a very hazardous place.

In this analogy, the train is the child, the conductor is the caregiver and the unforeseen accident is the trauma. Since train A had a caring conductor (child having a secure attachment with a caregiver), the train was fixed, continued as planned, and made it to its destination (child healed from the trauma, continued a healthy development, and learning resilience in the process). Since train B did not have a caring conductor (child having an unsecure attachment with a caregiver), the train remained damaged, continued on the wrong path, and received more damages (child not healing from trauma, being retraumatized and traumatizing others). The train never makes it to its destination, and instead, it ends up somewhere hazardous (child grows up to live an unhealthy lifestyle never finding happiness and their true purpose in life).

Understanding trauma and how it affects us is extremely important, not only for our development, but the development of our children.

This will explain how we got to where we are, and how to change where we're going. It can make all the difference in whether we have a healthy life or an unhealthy life. Whether we are a gift or a curse. Let's explore trauma more in depth to increase our understanding on this topic.

What is trauma?

Trauma is an event or set of circumstances experienced by an individual or group as physically and/or emotionally harmful or life-threatening with lasting effects. Trauma is a deeply distressing and disturbing experience. There are four main types of trauma; acute, chronic, complex and historical/intergenerational.

Acute trauma results from a single incident such as parents divorcing or rape. Chronic trauma is repeated and prolonged, such as domestic violence or sexual abuse. Complex trauma is exposure to multiple chronic traumatic events, often of an invasive and interpersonal (home or social) nature. Complex trauma takes place between the ages of 0-5 and it is caused by the adult who should have been caring for/protecting the child. Examples include neglect, physical abuse, and sexual abuse. Historical trauma is accumulative emotional and psychological pain over a lifespan, and across generations, as a result of a massive group trauma. An example of historical/inter-generational trauma would be the Black experience.

- Slavery: 1619
- Start of Policing/Slave Patrol Act: 1849
- Fugitive Slave Act: 1850
- The ratification of the 13th amendment: 1865
- Reconstruction Era (Black Code Laws): 1865-1877
- Jim Crow: 1877-1960's
- Poverty: 1930s-Present
- Mass Incarceration: 1900s-Present
- Police Brutality: 1849-Present

When it comes to identifying different types of trauma, you have the obvious traumas that most people come up with, but then you have the overlooked traumas that most people would consider "life". Some of the more obvious traumas would be abuse (verbal, physical, sexual, and neglect), assault (physical and sexual), natural disasters, grief (loss of loved one) being a victim of violent crime, an accident or medical illness, and war experiences. Some of the more overlooked traumas would be witnessing terror (real or cinematic), grief (loss of a pet or a break-up) being in foster care, incarceration, feeling unprotected, inferior or unloved, religion, parents showing favoritism, losing a job or can't find one, colorism, being a single mother, and being the child of a single mother. Below is a table depicting the different traumas reported by Black men about themselves.

* = reported by multiple Black men
• Grew up with men that believed a man's opinion mattered above all others in the home.

• Grew up without a father * 73%. Out of 73%
   o 23% specifically noted due to prison.
   o 27% had been incarcerated themselves.

• Raised by a single mother/grandmother.
• Raised in an abusive environment (verbally, emotionally and/or physically). *
• Someone in the immediate family went to prison. *
• Mother on Drugs/Alcoholic. *
• Women cheated on their boyfriends/husbands with them. *
• Been kicked out the house.
• Mother died during their early childhood. *

- Sexually abused by an older female or male before age 6 * 12%.
- Foster Care
- Emotionally Neglected *
- Been lied to or betrayed *
- Witnessing a death or murder *
- Been abused in relationships (verbally, physically and emotionally). *
- "Childhood was horrible!" (no details given).

Here are some statistics to show just how often and how many of us will experience or are currently experiencing trauma. 60% of adults reported experiencing abuse or other difficult family circumstances during childhood. 60% of youth aged 17 and younger reported five or more exposures to violence and abuse either directly or indirectly. 26% of children in the U.S will witness or experience a traumatic event before the age of four. Among 536 elementary and middle school children surveyed in an inner-city community, 30% had witnessed a stabbing and 26% had witnessed a shooting. 2% of all children experienced sexual assault or sexual abuse in 2019, with the rate at nearly 11% for girls aged 14 to 17. In one year, 39% of children between the ages of 12 and 17 reported witnessing violence. 17% reported being a victim of physical assault and 8% reported being the victim of sexual assault. Young children exposed to five or more significant adverse experiences in the first three years of childhood face a 76% likelihood of having one or more delays in their language or emotional development, due to the impact of trauma on the brain.

Impact of Trauma on the Brain

Stress is a feeling of emotional or physical tension from an event or thought. Stress is the body's natural reaction to challenges or demands. The goal of stress is to give your body the strength and energy it needs in order to protect you. Stress can be both positive (eustress) and negative (distress). Stress can be positive when it helps to protect you from real danger, prepares you for a new baby or helps you to accomplish a task. On the other hand, stress can be negative when it manifests severe anxiety which disrupts your ability to perform, prevents you from being able to cope, and causes mental and physical problems.

I would like you to participate in this activity to help visualize the structure of the brain in order to understand the impact of trauma.

- Hold your hand up like you are showing the number 5. Your forearm would be considered the spinal cord. The spinal cord receives input information from the outside world to help you survive and maintain bodily functions like walking or reflexes.

- Your wrist and the palm of your hand will be considered your brain stem. The brain stem controls the signals between the brain and body to promote survival. The brain stem controls breathing, swallowing, heart rate, blood pressure, and body temperature.

- Fold your thumb down as if to show the number four. Your thumb would be considered your amygdala. The amygdala is associated with all of your emotions. When you recall an emotional memory or experience an emotional event, your amygdala is activated, triggering your fight or flight responses.

- The last part is your cortex. Fold your remaining four fingers over your thumb; all four fingers are considered to be the cortex. The cortex is responsible for your thought process, perception, problem-solving and imagination. It's the part of the brain that regulates behavior by mediating conflicting thoughts, choosing between right and wrong and having the ability to have foresight. The cortex is also the part of the brain that develops last, and it does not become fully developed until about age 25.

The oldest part of the brain, is the reptilian brain; this is considered the brainstem. The second part of the brain is the limbic system; this is where your amygdala is located. The last part of the brain is your cortex. Despite the sophisticated evolution of the human brain, its primary function remains as self-preservation. Meaning, in times of threat or danger, your stress response system will activate; and at this time the reptilian brain and limbic system will over-ride the more logical and intellectual cortex.

The amygdala is the key part of the limbic system; it controls the brain's response to threat or danger by asking one simple question, "Is it safe?". The brain is designed to keep you alive. So, when the amygdala perceives a threat, it immediately sets off the brain's alarm system. At this point, your cortex shuts down and your amygdala activates your Fight, Flight or Freeze responses.

- Fight- Aggressive behaviors, to stand up to and survive.
- Flight- Run away to survive.
- Freeze- Hide or stop in your tracks/paralyzed to survive.

Once your fight or flight is activated (amygdala), your rational thought (cortex) is less possible at this time. Your brain will pump cortisol (a natural chemical to calm distress), and you will have a rush of adrenaline, causing increased heartrate, blood flow to muscles and an increase in respiration (brainstem). This process is called your stress response system and it is how your brain keeps you alive in the midst of danger.

Although this system is your brain's natural alarm system, like anything else in the body, it can also crash or malfunction. If the trauma experienced is prolonged and/or repetitive, it can cause your brain's alarm system to become jammed or no longer function properly. You will be in a constant state of alarm or arousal (experiencing high levels a negative stress), because your brain is unable to distinguish between actual danger (ie. physical abuse) and perceived danger (ie. normal relationship conflicts).

When your brain is stuck in a state of alarm, it constantly releases cortisol. In smaller doses, cortisol will work the way it is meant to; but in higher levels, it becomes a danger to the brain. Eventually, your brain will become less capable of handling stress. Your brain will create emotional and physical responses to the stress, which could result in emotional numbing or psychological avoidance. This will absolutely affect your sense of safety and security, diminishing your ability to trust others, and have healthy relationships.

Processing Session

This section may have been triggering for some. If this is the case, please take a break from reading and do some self-care

1. Ladies, do the traumas reported change your perspective of BM?
2. Moving forward, how will you use this knowledge when interacting with BM?
3. Fellas how does it feel to see that you aren't alone; that there are other BM who

share similar to the same experiences as you?

4. Were you aware that there was a difference between positive and negative stress?

5. Think of some events/thoughts you've had in your life that produced positive and negative stress. How did the positive stressors make your feel versus the negative stressors?

6. Take some time and identify your triggers (something or someone that causes you to feel strong emotions related to a memory or a flashback of a trauma). In what way do you respond when triggered in your relationships; flight, flight or freeze?

7. If prolonged or repetitive trauma can malfunction your stress response system (leaving you in a state of alarm) how does this directly affect you and others in the Black community?

8. Moving forward, what can you do to be more proactive regarding your triggers and emotional responses in your relationships and in life?

Chapter 8: Impact of Trauma Across a Lifespan

For a long time, mental health and trauma wasn't a topic that was discussed within the Black community. Despite all we have been through historically and personally, we were not encouraged to go to therapy. Instead, we are told "you're strong, you will get through it," "go to church and pray about it," or no-one said anything. In 2014, 18.8% of non-Hispanic white adults got mental health treatment or counseling, compared to just 9.4% of Black adults. Only recently has the topic of mental health and trauma been the focus of discussion within our communities. Thanks to individuals like Taraji P Henson, KeKe Palmer, Michelle Williams, Jada Pinkett-Smith, Amanda Seales, and Charlemagne Tha God, these discussions are becoming more prevalent and open among the masses. Although these discussions are more prevalent and open, it appears that they are being led more by Black women in the community than by Black men.

According to the feedback I received, 82% of Black men encourage seeking mental health support, but only 45% have actually sought support. When attempting to gather information from Black men regarding mental health, I noticed some level of discomfort, especially if there were other Black men around them during the discussion. There has been a huge taboo within our community regarding mental health as a whole, but an even bigger one specifically with Black men.

Historical Traumas

In chapter seven, the different types of traumas were discussed. One of the types mentioned was historical/intergenerational trauma. I made a general list of some of our historical traumas, but in this chapter, I will go into more detail about a few of them. My goal is to help give more perspective on just how traumatizing our history was, and how it still greatly affects us today.

In 1619, the legal institution of human chattel first began. Black people worked the fields from sunup to sundown and were being treated way beyond less than human. So many of the enslaved died at the hands of white slave owners, that in 1669, Virginia passed a law called The Casual Killing Act. "If any slave resists his master (or any other by his master's order correcting him), and by the extremity of the correction should he die, that his death shall not be a felony."

In 1831, Nat Turner and 6 others led a two-day rebellion against slavery, killing 55 white people, and in 1849, Harriet Tubman escaped and began her journey via the underground railroad. Also, in 1849, was the beginning of policing and a year later, in 1850, the second Fugitive Slave Act was passed. The start of policing was called the Slave Patrol Act, and their 3 main goals were to return runaway slaves, inflict so much terror that the enslaved were too scared to rebel, and to maintain "discipline" on the plantation. The second Fugitive Slave Act authorized local governments to seize and return runaway slaves to their owners, and imposed penalties on anyone who aided in their flight.

In 1865, the 13th amendment was ratified. Neither slavery nor involuntary servitude shall exist within the United States, or any place subject to their jurisdiction <u>except as a punishment for crime</u>. After the Civil War, slavery persisted in the form of convict leasing, a system that leased prisoners to **private** railways, mines, and large plantations. Some of the crimes that landed Black men back into slavery was malicious mischief, being unemployed or associating with an unemployed person, misspending their earnings, insulting gestures, preaching the gospel without a license, and land ownership.

According to Michelle Alexander, after the Civil War in 1863, new offenses like "malicious mischief" were vague and could be a felony or a misdemeanor depending on the supposed behavior. These laws sent Black men to prison more than before and by the late 19th century the country experienced its first prison boom. While states profited, prisoners earned no pay and faced inhumane, dangerous, and often deadly work conditions.

From 1877-1964, Jim Crow was implemented; a body of law that institutionalized economic, social, and educational disadvantages for Black people. The laws mandated segregation of schools, parks, libraries, drinking fountains, restrooms, buses, trains, and restaurants; "Whites Only" and "Colored Only." These laws ensured white superiority. During this period of time, danger was a regular aspect of Black life. Black schools were vandalized and destroyed, sometimes with people inside. Groups of violent white people attacked, tortured, and lynched Black people in the night. Families were also attacked and forced off their land all across the South. Also, during this time, the Ku Klux Klan was active. This ruthless domestic terroristic organization, terrorized and murdered Black people throughout the South. A new 2020 study, brings the number of Black victims of racial terror killings by the Ku Klux Klan between 1865-1950 to almost 6,500.

The history that has been discussed thus far is by no means even a fraction of what has actually taken place, yet the things mentioned have had a huge impact on us today. The prison system today is an exact replica of the convict leasing program. Today, Black men are still being, wrongfully convicted and their sentence is disproportionately longer than that of white men. It is a fact that Black men make up the largest percentage of the prison population, and their presence in these **privatized** **prisons** provide this country with a way to continue using Black bodies for commodity and disposal. Black men are in prison making clothing, furniture, car parts, dentures, lingerie, toys, and a whole lot more for free. *While this country profits, prisoners earn no pay and are faced with inhumane, dangerous, and often deadly work conditions.* The criminal justice system was, and still is, strategically employed to force Black people into the system of repression and control. Without systematic change, this a tactic will continue to be successful for generations to come.

The slave patrol, being the start of policing, shines a light on the current state of policing today. Police officers have a track record for not only using illegal tactics to wrongfully arrest

Black people, but also for violating the rights of Black people via excessive force. Sometimes, police are so excessive that Black people end up dead; and to make it worse, their murderers walk free. The casual killing act of 1669 was a law that protected white slave owners from being charged with murder for the killing of a Black man, woman, or child via "correcting them." This can be seen as the same as white police officers getting off for the killings of unarmed Black people today.

In 1964, the Civil Rights Act was passed. This law ended segregation in public places and banned employment discrimination on the basis of race, color, religion, sex, or national origin. This is known as one of the crowning legislative achievements of the civil rights movement. This country went from making it illegal for Black people to read, to allowing whites and the KKK to burn down Black schools with Black children inside, to now allowing Black students and white students to learn together, equally. This could probably be a good thing if it was actually true. The Civil Rights Act gave the powers that be, control over the education of Black children, creating what we now know to be, "the school to prison pipeline."

In 2001, the No Child Left Behind Act was signed into law. This law required students to be tested yearly in reading and math, in grades 3rd to 8th, and once in high school. Students were to meet standards set by the state, and if a school failed to show progress, then they faced cut-offs in public funding. In order for schools to properly educate their students, they require adequate resources such as appropriate materials, curriculum and smaller class sizes. When these concerns were brought up, the response given was "We don't have funding for that."

Today, we have 79% of Black 4th through 8th graders who are not proficient in reading or math. Because Black children are not being properly educated, they now have a high number of ADHD and Special Education labels. Black students are suspended or expelled 3 times more than white students. While Black students make up 16% of the public-school enrollment, they account for 42% of all students who have been suspended multiple times. 31% of Black students represent school-related arrests, and Black students suspended or expelled for discretionary violations are nearly 3 times more likely to be in contact with the juvenile justice system, the following year.

In 2014, Black youth were 14% of the youth's population, but 52.5% of the youth transferred to adult court by juvenile court judges. In the criminal justice system, there is a term called Direct File. Direct File occurs when a prosecutor is given the power to file charges against a juvenile in adult criminal court. Prosecutors are not only allowed to direct file youth to adult court, but bypass the review of the juvenile court judge in the process. They have the power to override any juvenile or family court's jurisdiction over a case. California is a state that, up until 2016, prosecutors had the option to direct file. In California, Black youth were 11.3 times more likely to be direct filed than their white peers. From 2003 to 2018, more than 11,500 youth ages 14 to 17 were moved into adult courts across California. Kamala Harris was the DA of San Francisco from 2004 -2011, and the Attorney General of the state of California from 2011-2017. She is now vice president elect of the United States of America.

Due to the multigenerational trauma that Black people have endured, there's been a development of what Dr. Joy DeGruy calls "Post

Traumatic Slave Syndrome". Post Traumatic Slave Syndrome is a condition that exists when a population has experienced multigenerational trauma, resulting from centuries of slavery, and continues to experience oppression and institutionalized racism today. PTSS explains the cause behind many of the adaptive survival behaviors in Black communities throughout the United States.

Black people have developed an element of internalized oppression, and an extreme level of learned helplessness. They believe that the benefits of the society in which they live are not accessible to them. Distrust and suspicion exist within the Black community, which, at times, leads to a display of different forms of violence towards one another. The communities are overwhelmed with feelings of depression and hopelessness, which can account for the self-destructive outlook. And when faced with events of injustice that mimic trauma from the past, it leaves Black people in a frozen state of terror, too scared to fight back for fear of either death or imprisonment.

Personal Traumas

In 1998, the Adverse Childhood Experience Study (ACEs) was published by the CDC. ACEs refers to a range of events that a child can experience, which leads to chronic stress responses. Data was collected between 1995-1997, from 17,000 members who completed surveys on their childhood experiences and current health status and behaviors. Although there are many sources of childhood trauma, the researchers decided to focus on physical, emotional, and sexual abuse/neglect; and households with mental illness, domestic violence, divorce/separation, substance abuse, and incarceration.

The ACEs study asked 10 questions, with each question counting as 1 point. 64% reported at least one ACE. More than one in five reported three or more ACEs, and 12% reported four or more ACEs. The ACEs study uncovered a stunning link between childhood trauma and the chronic diseases people develop as adults. The higher the ACEs number, the higher the risk. Some physical effects include heart disease, cancer, autoimmune diseases, diabetes, smoking, and obesity. Some emotional effects include poor self-image, nervousness, anxiety, anger, self-pity, depression, and suicidal behaviors. I can assume, right now you are thinking about everyone you know (including yourself) that has presented or is currently presenting the effects mentioned above. You are probably wondering if it was caused by trauma. Although I cannot personally answer this question, according to the CDC, at least 5 of the top 10 leading causes of death are associated with ACEs.

An ACE score of 3 or more is considered high. If you have a high ACE score, you are 2 times more likely to become a smoker, and 7 times more likely to become an alcoholic. You are 2 times more likely to get Hepatitis, 4 ½ times more likely to become depressed, and 12 times more likely to try to die by suicide. When one has an ACE score of 6 or more, you cut 20 years off your life expectancy. Knowing your ACE score means understanding the risks, and being able to prevent the possible consequences.

As stated in an earlier chapter, there is nothing more emotionally exhausting for a healthy BW than trying to unconditionally love a Black man that doesn't know how to be loved and doesn't know how to love in return. I will discuss the ACEs and additional traumas of four different unhealthy BM. I will explain how their traumas essentially destroyed their relationships with healthy BW and not only victimized those women in the process, but revictimized themselves as well.

When reading this chapter, remember that these are the personal stories of four individual men. This chapter is by no means a formula for how specific traumas will affect a specific individual. These are examples of how their traumas affected their relationships. How your traumas impact you and your relationships may look different. For confidentiality purposes, they will remain anonymous and will be referred to by a name that fits the effects of their traumas.

Mr. Barbaric

Mr. Barbaric is what you would consider "the bad boy." He was born and raised in the inner city with his Aunt as his guardian. His father was in jail for murder, and his mother died when he was young. Although he is considered a bad boy, he had some very special hidden talents. He could draw exceptionally well. He was a great writer and a very good actor. Unfortunately, his upbringing in the streets led him far away from his talents and soon enough, street pharmaceuticals became his occupation of choice. He was known for protecting and providing for the women in his family. He had the utmost love and respect for them, but sadly that respect didn't always extend to women outside his family.

Being in "the lifestyle," he was very popular with the ladies. This man got any and everything he wanted, regardless of how he spoke to them or what he did to them. He had three children by two different mothers, and of course they fought over him. When he got himself locked up, he was very much taken care of, sometimes by women with husbands and boyfriends. Women would answer his jail calls while their man was in the bed or in the next room asleep. I guess there's some truth to the saying, "girls love a bad boy."

Unexpectedly, he fell in love; with a girl he had known for a few years. He always had a thing for her, but she was the one girl who "didn't take his shit." He knew she was different and the street life wouldn't be OK with her. She initially opposed the idea, but he swore he was serious, so she gave him a shot. In the beginning, it was all unicorns, rainbows, and butterflies. They were very much in love with one another but it didn't last. He was loyal, protective, and provided, but being respectful was a struggle.

Whenever he would get upset or angry, Mr. Barbaric would show up. He would mentally and verbally abuse her, and somehow blame her for his behavior. Some examples include telling her she was borderline fat and saying, "Why can't you do what I want you to do, to be how I was you to be? You gonna force me look for what I want somewhere else." When she would encourage him to stop yelling and degrading her, he would respond with, "It's your fault. If you didn't do the stupid stuff you do then I wouldn't get mad." When she would suggest better ways for them to resolve their issues, he would reply, "This shit stupid! Who talks like this?"

One day, he got upset with her because she had an opinion about something and he didn't agree with it. This led to him hanging up on her. Before the line disconnected, he said to a friend "F**k this b**ch, she can go kill herself." One of the last things he said to her before she left the relationship for good was "Man, you tripping. You not gonna find one relationship where a man ain't beating, cheating, or being verbally abusive. At least I ain't beating on you or cheating on you. This is as good as you gonna get." When she said she would rather be alone than to be with him, his last words were, "Get out my car…and send me an invitation to the wedding when you find your Mr. Perfect."

Mr. Emotionally Unavailable

Mr. Emotionally Unavailable is what you would consider "the hero." He was born to an alcoholic mother, and was raised in the Southern country ghettos; he never knew his father. At the age of four, he was removed from the home due to child neglect and was placed in foster care. In foster care, he was sexually abused by the couple's son before being placed back in his mother's care via his grandmother. Although he lived with his grandmother, his mother was still very much around. So much so, that one day, they were out shopping, and due to her neglect, he was hit by a car and had to be airlifted to the hospital. When he woke up in the hospital, there was no one there; he was only 5 years old at the time.

His childhood featured his alcoholic mother and her deadbeat boyfriends. Growing up, he and his mother would be in the home together, but they would never say a word to each other. It was like they were home alone. When he managed to relocate and began a new life, he vowed to never return. He lived with his Aunt and his two cousins. While he stayed there, he made sure he worked, contributed, and showed appreciation to his Aunt for allowing him to stay there. Unfortunately, this was short-lived. His aunt kicked him out of the house due to jealousy.

Later, he got married, but his marriage was just as toxic as his childhood. His wife was verbally, mentally, and physically abusive. She would verbally abuse him by telling him he was nothing and useless. She would emotionally abuse him by saying, "That's why you got molested." She would also physically abuse him by hitting him with an open and closed fist, or with objects. This went on for a period of 10 years before he finally was able to walk away, get a divorce, and get custody of their child.

He moved on and began to do things that brought him joy, such as singing and attending speech competitions. He valued education and ensured that his child didn't fall victim to the school to prison pipeline. He was always helping people, especially women. Anytime a person needed help with anything, he was there to save the day. He was always going out of his way to be helpful, leaving a positive impression on the people he helped. The only problem with this was that some of the women he tried to help ended up becoming verbally and physically aggressive towards him.

When he decided to date again, he met a woman who he thought was quite amazing; someone very different from the woman he was married to for ten years. He always made these grand gestures; he sent flowers to her job, bought her little cute gifts and spent time with her. For one of their dates, he laid rose petals out from the door to the car, and put a necklace around her neck before she got in. He was always very sweet, respectful, and attentive. On Valentine's day, he showered her with more gifts, and they still hadn't even had their first kiss.

Once they grew closer and actually began to build a connection, things suddenly changed; Mr. Emotional Unavailable arrived. He grew distant. First with texts and calls, and then with in-person contact. The woman he was with was very confused and very hurt; she thought they had a connection. When she approached him with her hurt, this made matters worse. He would tell her, "You're acting irrational. Why do you have these strong emotions?" It was like the three months they spent together completely disappeared. This infuriated her, how could he just throw all that time away like it didn't matter?

During the course of this back and forth, she was able to see how he was as a parent, and she quickly noticed the odd relationship dynamic between him and his child. They never said good morning or goodnight. During the day, they barely talked to each other at all. When they did talk, it was about school or the child's mother. They barely played together, spent time together, or even hugged. There was absolutely no connection.

He was also excessively hard on his child; nothing was ever good enough. If his child passed a test, getting 8 out of 10 correct, he would focus on the 2 wrong answers. Whenever he felt the need to "discipline" his child, he would use both verbal and physical aggression. One time, his child decided to eat some candy one morning, instead of actual breakfast, and he responded with "Why do you have to be so stupid. I didn't raise you to be stupid. I raised you to have common sense. I should punch you in your f**king chest." Another time, his child removed his charger from his room without permission and when he came to get it, he snatched it back, towered over his child and glared for about 5 secs before walking away. The woman he was dating tried to encourage healthier ways of parenting, but to no avail. The toxicity not only continued, but worsened; prompting them to go their separate ways.

Mr. Defensive

Mr. Defensive is what you would consider "the nice guy." He was born and raised in a small-town ghetto up North, where he lived with his mother and his siblings. He grew up without his father due to incarceration. Due to the breakdown of his family, he had to take on the role as the "man of the house," even though he wasn't the oldest. Although he was the one to help keep the household together, he was always told that what he did was never good enough, and he never felt favored or appreciated. These comments didn't just happen in the home, but from others outside his home as well. Since he took on the role as "man of the house," he ended up having to get a job to help contribute to the household. At one of the jobs he worked at, he was told that he was slow and that he would never make it. He was picked on for a lack of bass in his voice, and he wasn't taken seriously. No-one believed that he would go to college, let alone graduate.

Growing up, he didn't have the best experiences with women. Whenever he would talk to a girl and introduce her to his friends, they always seemed to fall for his friends. It got to the point where he would rather hide the woman he was dating than introduce her to his friends for fear of them losing interest in him. At times, he seemed to be the odd ball out; going out with his friends, but never getting the same female attention as them. He was always seen as the nice guy; a good friend when you needed one.

Having been told he would never amount to nothing, in conjunction with feeling robbed, regarding the women he liked liking his friends, he didn't have the highest self-esteem. When walking to and from his destinations, he would see other men driving nice cars and getting the girls. This also contributed to his feelings of inadequacy. Eventually, he decided to relocate and start fresh in a new place.

Being in a new place without his old friends opened the door for a new him, and new relationship possibilities. As the years passed, he managed to build the life he wanted. He got the job, the car, and the apartment, but his lady was still nowhere to be found. He was a great cook, very attentive to women, and he craved partnership. He was always doing different forms of acts of service. If a female friend called him drunk and needed a ride, he would pick her up. If a female friend needed a place to stay because she was in a bad situation, he would offer his place. He would cook and offer a female friend to come eat, or take a plate to her. He would always go out of his way to attend to a woman. So, why hadn't a relationship ever formed from his dating experiences?

When it came to dating, he always seemed to find women he was interested in, but the feelings weren't always reciprocated. When he did find a woman that was interested in him, she was either interested because she had broken up with her boyfriend or he was too busy comparing the one that liked him, to the one he liked. "Can she take my mind off these other girls?" is a question he would ask himself.

One time, he managed to find a woman that he was really interested in. During the course of getting to know each other, she learned that he had a huge problem with accepting help and taking advice or constructive criticism. Whenever she would suggest something or try to help, Mr. Defensive would show up and fight for his life. For example, he made a phone call to AT&T to discuss an app he was being charged for, but didn't sign up for. While on speakerphone, in her presence, she overheard the representative explain that the app showing was a generic picture, and that what he was being charged for was an app he actually purchased. He didn't understand, so, she attempted to try and explain it to him. He responded with "I got it I got it…I can handle it." When he hung up, he proceeded to say that he was "handling his business" and usually, when someone is handling business, the other person shouldn't involve themselves. Another time, he was asked if he could go make sure she had locked the doors to the car. He was given the key and she proceeded to say, "You don't have to go all the way out there; you can check from the patio door." Before she could finish the sentence, he interrupted with a slight bit of aggression saying "I got it…I'm not an idiot."

During this time period, he wasn't in the best position financially. He was barely able to keep the electricity on, put gas in his car, his cell phone was turned off, and overdraft fees was becoming his best friend. At first, she was not aware of his financial situation. She didn't find out until she asked him to go to her house and he said he couldn't, and had to explain why. "If I come to your house, I won't have enough gas to get to work." Hearing about him being in this extreme financial bind would not have been a problem, except for the fact that he made sure the cable was on so he could watch Power, and the Wi-Fi was on to accommodate whoever was using his internet at the time.

At first, she didn't say anything to him about his finances, but when he started to check his account before he went to the store each time, she could no longer hold her tongue. She attempted to talk to him about it and tried to help better focus his priorities and problem solve, but his response was, "Well, this is my personal business, and I don't think it's appropriate for people to discuss their personal finances with others." After a while, this same song and dance became more and more intolerable. Eventually, she decided to go her separate way.

Mr. Catastrophizing

Mr. Catastrophizing is what you would consider "the good guy." Although he was born and raised in the inner city, the growth mindset of his parents allowed him to experience life on the other side of the tracks. He spent a lot of his childhood going to school in the suburban areas. He was very much exposed to extracurricular activities the average Black boy wouldn't have access to or participate in. His first relationship was with his childhood sweetheart; they had a very special bond. Both were virgins while they dated a few years, and lost their virginities to each other. Throughout the years, he became known for showing the utmost respect to women. Any woman that had the opportunity to get to know him or date him never wanted it any other way.

Although his upbringing was way different from that of the average Black boy in the hood, it still didn't stop him from being sucked into "the lifestyle." For him, the street life was a gift and a curse. At first, he was living what he thought was his best life. He was making money, spending money, and having a good time in the process. Although the lifestyle came with women, he wasn't the type to mess around with different women all the time. If he was single, he had his fun, but if he was in a relationship, he was 100% committed and faithful.

Eventually, his fun turned to misery when he decided to try the drug he was selling. For 5 years, he fought his addiction, while simultaneously selling drugs. In the lifestyle, he had seen things like watching someone die, and had done things while high off his own supply. He soon grew tired of the fight and decided enough was enough. He went home, got clean, and completely turned his life around.

Over the next few years, he would live his new sober life and date in the process. Although he was a good guy, he didn't always have the best experience with women. There was something about him that could make a woman feel really special and risk it all. He spent a lot of time being with women who were already in relationships. Women were cheating on their husbands and boyfriends with him. Eventually, his conscience caught up with him and he decided he would no longer participate in their infidelities.

After making this decision, it opened the door for him to reconnect with his high school sweetheart. At this time, they were in different states, but their reconnection prompted her to relocate about a year later. He was so happy and excited to be back with his first love, but sadly, it was short-lived. About a month after the move, she began to show signs of not being happy. Not unhappy with him, but unhappy with being in a new place without her family and friends. She eventually went back home. Although he supported whatever was best for her, he was left severely heart broken. He spent a year rebuilding his relationship with his first love, only to have it end a month after she moved.

About 2 years later, he reconnected with a woman he had a crush on in the past. He was very excited and very adamant about maintaining contact, especially since she lived out of state. Initially, they started off as friends, just catching up and reminiscing. However, over time, it naturally progressed into more. As the long-distance relationship developed, so did the problems; Mr. Catastrophizing arrived.

At first, it started out light. He would say things like, "You better not be playing around because I'm serious about you," "I hope you not lying to me," or "What's wrong with you? You seem too good to be true." As time passed, it progressed into something more severe. One night, right before they hung up, she said "Goodnight," and he responded with "Goodnight, you better not be calling no one else after we hang up."

In another situation, she made a last-minute appointment to the nail salon and sent a quick text saying "Hey, I just made a last-minute appointment for 6pm, if I don't answer, it's because I can't," then she jumped in the shower. When she got out and checked her phone, he had sent two messages. "What is the appointment" and then two minutes later, he sent another messages that said, "Fine. Whatever. I guess I'll talk to you after your NEW appointment." Another time she got a call from a male friend who had experienced a death in the family and needed to talk. She explained that she needed to take the call. At first, he seemed understanding, but when the friend called back a second time, he said, "Man I'mma just talk to you tomorrow." One of the major incidences that took place was when she explained that before they were to become intimate, she wanted to get tested for STDs and HIV, and wanted him to do the same. His response was "I can't believe you. You must think I have something or had something. You clearly don't trust me. I would never ask you to do this." He refused to answer her calls for 2 days.

Eventually, it became too much and she tried to resolve it with him. When she tried to prompt the conversation, he would immediately respond with agitation. "Omg! Come on. Can we please not talk about this?" Whenever she did manage to get him to discuss the issues, he would automatically say, "Listen, just tell me if you don't want to do this. If you don't want to be with me, just tell me now." No matter how many times it was explained to him that she wasn't interested in leaving, he always resorted to it. So much so that he would completely disconnect sometimes, refusing to talk or answer the phone. This toxicity soon led to the demise of the relationship.

Connecting the Dots

Mr. Barbaric

His Traumas
- Acute: Death of his mother
- Complex: Father in jail
- Chronic: Father in jail. Street Life and Incarceration

ACEs Score: 3

Impact on Relationship
- What destroyed the relationship was his perception and his inability to control strong emotions. Being raised in the streets, he developed a very cold and harsh way of expressing his emotions. Respect was not required for street pharmaceutical transactions.
- When dealing with women, even though he spoke to them with a great deal of disrespect, it never made a difference. The women in his life still catered to him despite his display of disrespectful behaviors.

He essentially learned that he can say whatever he wanted, do whatever he wanted and still get whatever he wanted.

- Additionally, he found the transition from being illegal to legal hard, especially on his pride as a man. Whenever she would hold him accountable for following through with his plans or encourage different ways of solving their problems, it would cause him high levels of frustrations.

- Being in this position activated his fight or flight response system. In order to start all the way over and react differently than before, you have to humble yourself, admit that there is a problem, and walk the path to change. Unfortunately, being humble was a skill he had not learned yet, leading to an internal battle within himself where he took his frustrations out on her instead (fight). It wasn't that he didn't love her, he just couldn't control his emotions. In the end, he lost his first love and had to live with the regrets of how he treated her.

Mr. Emotionally Unavailable

His Traumas

- Acute:
- Complex: Sexual Abuse, Neglect, and Alcoholic Mother
- Chronic: Father Unknown, Domestic Violence, Poverty, Abandonment, and Alcoholic Mother

ACEs Score: 7

Impact on Relationship

- What destroyed the relationship was his inability to trust and connect. Having been neglected and sexually abused before the age of 5, set the precedent that no-one close to him could be trusted. This was solidified later in his adult years when he was verbally and physically abused by his wife of 10 years and other female friends he tried to help. He essentially learned that connection was unsafe and people could not be trusted.

- Everything about him was robotic, just an empty shell living a day-to-day routine. He had created a mask and learned to show the world the man he wanted to be. But a mask can only last for so long; eventually the real person will be seen.

- The moment he felt a connection with the woman he was dating, he perceived that he was in danger and his fight/flight was activated. Once he believed he was in danger, he immediately disassociated himself from her (flight). He was unable to see that he was actually safe with her and that she was not like those other women.

- Her strong emotional responses didn't help. Even though her reactions weren't irrational, they were too strong for him. He associated her emotions with that of the abusive women he'd been with previously. To him, strong emotions equaled verbal and physical aggression.

- The worst part about all of this, is that, he will pass down the effects of his traumas to his child. His child has not only learned unhealthy ways to resolve conflicts, but also how to live day to day without interactions or affection. Sadly, the cycle will continue.

Mr. Defensive

His Traumas
- Acute:

- Complex: Father incarcerated
- Chronic: Verbal/Mental Abuse, Poverty, Father incarcerated, Overlooked, and Parent showing favoritism

ACEs Score: 4

Impact on Relationship

- There were a few contributing factors that destroyed the potential of this relationship. The first was having been told, over the course of years, that he was slow and would never amount to anything. The second was his relationship inexperience and his refusal to learn.

- Having been robbed of relationships created two problems. The first was a feeling of insecurity because the girls he was interested in were more interested in his friends. The second was lacking the understanding of how to connect with a woman. Even though he was extremely sweet, considerate and attentive, he still had important things to learn in regards to relationships. A woman wasn't able to teach him because he interpreted his lack of knowledge in certain things as "I'm slow."

- Having been told he would never amount to nothing or have nothing, put him in a position to feel like he needed to prove himself. He viewed success in things such as a job, car, clothes, and a place to live. When he established all of the above and still had no luck finding his soulmate, this too added to his thought of "what am I doing wrong?"

- The moment the woman he was dating had given any type of advice, criticism, or "help," it triggered his fight or flight response. He immediately associated these things with being called slow and not knowing. This caused him to become irrationally defensive (fight). He was unable to see that she wasn't calling him slow, she was just simply trying to help him. In the end, he was left alone...again.

Mr. Catastrophizing

His Traumas
- Acute: Broken Heart and Witnessing a death
- Complex:

- Chronic: Street Life, Incarceration, Drug use, and Infidelities

ACEs Score: 3

Impact on Relationship

- What destroyed the relationship was his inability to challenge his negative thoughts and regulate his emotions. Having been in the streets selling and doing drugs, he was exposed to and experienced the worst that lifestyle had to offer. He developed this "I will get you before you get me" mindset.

- Having been in multiple situations with women who have cheated on their boyfriends or husbands with him left him seeing women as untrustworthy. In addition, with having his heartbroken by his childhood sweetheart, he was left always thinking of the worst possible outcome.

- Although the woman he was dating gave him no reason to believe he couldn't trust her, he still managed to directly and indirectly accuse her of being disloyal. No matter how many times it was shown to him that his way of thinking was irrational, he could not help but think the worst.

- With the woman he was dating being out of state, this also contributed to him thinking the worst. Not knowing what she was doing when they weren't on the phone left an opportunity for his mind to wander. Also, due to his childhood sweetheart returning back home, after only a month with him left him feeling apprehensive. He could only think that the same would happen with the current woman he was dating.

- Whenever the woman he was dating tried to problem solve a conflict with him, he would automatically think she wanted to end the relationship. Since this woman was very different from his past relationships, he never truly trusted her. He would question it; "Is this too good to be true?" He was always waiting for her to flip the switch and change.

- Whenever he would experience these negative thoughts, he would become overwhelmed with stress, and his fight/flight would automatically activate. He would shut down, hang-up, refuse to answer the phone or respond saying, "tell me if you don't want to be with me" (flight). Even though he knew that the woman he was dating was different from the others, his thoughts wouldn't allow him to believe it. His thoughts were so intrusive that he would in turn create chaos and sabotage the relationship himself; reexperiencing a broken heart.

In forensic psychology, I first learned about serial killers and discovered that they all experienced severe traumatic childhoods. Highlighting their traumatic childhoods is not an excuse for their behaviors, just an explanation for how they developed into serial killers. Now, you're probably thinking to yourself right now "What is she talking about, and what do serial killers have to do with anything?" Well, here is the connection. Due to the historical and personal traumas that Black people have endured over the years, they have become what I like to call "emotional serial killers." Instead of killing people physically like serial killers do, they kill people emotionally.

When you have experienced traumatic events and have not healed, you cannot proceed to have a healthy relationship; you will be unsuccessful. Your traumas will present themselves in different aspects of the relationship, creating drama and toxicity. As discussed, it doesn't matter if both or one of you is unhealthy, everyone will be victimized; destroying themselves and others around them.

Overall, it is important for both Black men and women to understand their historical and personal traumas as this will help them to heal and evolve. My personal belief is that when it comes to Black men, it is extremely important that they understand what their traumas are, and how they directly impact their ability to live and have healthy relationships. It is also equally important for them to be comfortable with speaking honestly about it and seeking appropriate mental health support. Black men are our leaders and being knowledgeable and healthy are key ingredients to leading.

Processing Session

This section may have been triggering for some. If this is the case, please take a break from reading and take time to self-care

1. Do you have an understanding of how our historical traumas still have an impact on us today?

2. Do you think you suffer from internalized racism or learned helplessness? Why or Why not?

3. Did you vote for Kamala Harris? If so, how do you feel about that decision now?

4. How will you move forward to ensure that you and your descendants, will no longer be victims of systematic conditioning?

5. If you consider yourself "conscious," what will you do to ensure your descendants don't fall victim to systematic conditioning?

6. What is your ACE score? Go to the link below to find out:
   a. https://stopabusecampaign.org/what-are-adverse-childhood-experiences/what-is-your-ace-score/

7. According to the CDC, what chronic diseases are you at risk of developing? Have you developed any already?

8. Take some time and identify as many of your personal traumas as you can. Remember that there are three types; acute, chronic, and complex. Which ones do you

think have had the biggest impact on your life?

9. How have those traumas affected your ability to have healthy relationships? How?

10. If you could have a chance to do things differently, what would you have done?

11. Moving forward, what will you do to ensure you are not being an emotional serial killer or a victim of an emotional serial killer?

Part V: Healing Process

Quiet the Storm

Heavy Heart
Stomach in knots
Unable to function properly
with these racing thoughts

Can I Trust?
Is it Safe?
Should I try Again?

I tell myself yes
But then
Here comes the emotional
whirlwind

Fighting, running away
or completely shutting down
Plagued with past demons
left in my tears to drown

My mind and body keeping
score
Of all the memories from
before
I can't think
I can't sleep
I can no longer ignore

Exhausted by the toxicity
Tired of being scorned
No more hurt
No more pain
I'm ready to transform

But first
I must quiet the storm

Don't worry you're safe
is what I tell myself
Facing my past is essential
to healing my mental health

This process is hard
overwhelming
and draining
But as I feel this weight
release
I eventually stop
complaining

I've never felt so liberated
unchained or free
From now on
I welcome growth and
healing
On my journey

But this isn't just for me
I want all my people to be
free
Cleansing their minds and
bodies
From all that toxicity

I will encourage others to
welcome their healing
and transform
I think it's time for them too
to
Quiet the Storm

Queen X
10/28/2020

Chapter 9 ACEs and Resiliency

As previously explained, ACEs are traumatic events that occur in childhood and they can have a serious impact across one's lifespan. In order to effectively deal with the impact of ACEs and other traumas, building resilience is a must. Resilience is the ability to overcome a challenge and become healthy again. Now, you're probably thinking that because you've survived your traumas, then that means you have overcome them. Unfortunately, this is not true. If you have categorized yourself in the unhealthy category in the earlier chapters, then you have not learned resilience, but survival.

One of the main effects of ACEs and other traumas that greatly impact your ability to have resilience is depression. Depression is another topic that gets swept under the rug within the Black community, especially with Black men. Even though it exists within our homes, our communities, and our music, Black men have the hardest time saying "I am depressed." Is it because they don't want to admit it? Is it because they see it as a weakness? Or is it because they don't even know they are depressed? According to the data I received, the answer to all three questions is "yes." Some Black men view depression as a sign of weakness, some ignore it and continue to live, while others don't even realize they are experiencing depression. Since depression directly impacts your ability to be resilient; it's important to discuss what depression is, what can cause depression, and how to identify when you are depressed.

Depression

The clinical definition for depression is a mental health disorder characterized by a persistently depressed mood or loss of interest in activities, causing significant impairment in your daily life. Some of the reported causes of depression include abuse, conflicts with family or friends, death of a loved one or a major life change like losing a job/income, moving, or getting a divorce. According to the data I received, some of the reported causes of depression in Black men were past military experiences, not being able to provide for himself or his family, feelings of inadequacy "Am I doing enough? Do I spend enough time with my kids and family?", feeling trapped in a toxic relationship, feeling unloved or unappreciated by family, or within a relationship, having his child(ren) kept from him and feeling powerless to do anything about it, child support garnishments even though he takes care of his children, going to and coming home from prison, death/murder of a loved one, and being around negativity and negative energy.

The effects of depression are caused by an influx of cortisol, which enlarges and activates the amygdala; the part of the brain that controls your emotions and your fight or flight responses.

When your amygdala is more active due to depression, it can disrupt your sleep, appetite, energy levels, concentration, self-esteem, and create thoughts of suicide. While reviewing the data, I noticed two different signs of depression in Black men; some were signs of internalizing and others were externalizing. The internalizing signs included wearing dark colors, unable to have happy thoughts, loss of creativity or motivation, bottling everything up until it led to anxiety, panic attacks or a trip to the hospital for severe constipation, or other ailments, spending more time alone, neglecting personal hygiene or other responsibilities, oversleeping, loss of sex drive or appetite, and thoughts of suicide. The externalizing signs included having a sudden change in mood or attitude, easily agitated by things they weren't bothered by before, lashing out at whoever/whenever, being verbally or physically aggressive towards others, welcoming to risky situations, increase in sexual activity with multiple partners, and self-medicating with drugs or alcohol (weed and over the counter drugs included).

Although the focus was on Black men, depression is a mental health disorder that is pervasive and impacts everyone. It has been predicted that by 2030, depression will be the largest cause of early death or disability in any given age group. It is not only extremely important to be able to identify when you are depressed and what events led to your feelings of depression, but also how to combat feelings of depression by building strong resiliency skills.

Resiliency

Protective factors help a child and adult feel safe more quickly after experiencing the toxic stress of an adversity. Resiliency is a protective factor and a powerful antidote to combat depression. Resiliency is made up of five pillars; self-awareness, mindfulness, self-care, positive relationships and purpose. By strengthening these pillars, you become more resilient so that when you experience stress, you will be able to maintain a sense of balance and well-being.

Five Pillars

Self-Awareness

Self-awareness is having a clear understanding of who you are as a person; your strengths, weaknesses, feelings, and behaviors. Being self-aware is when you are able to identify your triggers (those things or people that cause you to feel strong emotions), and develop a healthier and more productive way of responding. Developing self-awareness is important for three reasons. First, because it will allow you to identify what you do well and what you need to work on. Second, you will be strengthening your ability to regulate your emotions. Third, you will experience higher levels of happiness, and higher levels of happiness increase your ability to be resilient.

Mindfulness

Mindfulness is the state of being conscious or fully aware of your feelings, thoughts, and bodily sensations. Purposefully paying attention. Practicing mindfulness will allow you to become fully present in the moment. Being able to completely experience or process a situation by way of your five senses (sight, smell, taste, touch, and sound), without judgement or distraction. This skill involves breathing techniques, guided imagery, or meditation to relax the mind and body. By learning mindfulness skills, you can use this as a healthy way to reduce stress and increase happiness.

Self-Care

Self-care is the ability to be mindful of your own needs and provide yourself with the necessary support when needed. It is taking the time to intentionally meet your own physical, mental, spiritual, or emotional needs. It requires your active engagement. Sacrificing your own needs and happiness for work, parents, children, friends, or family may "sound" honorable, but in the end, it leaves you empty, unfulfilled, and resentful. Taking care of your own needs first, puts you in a position to better support, or distance yourself from, those around you. Practicing self-care acts as a protective factor for your overall health. It allows you to deal with life's daily stressors without becoming consumed by them.

Positive Relationships

Relationships are the heart of humanity. Everything that's important about life, you learn in the context of a relationship. Positive relationships are social relations that make positive contributions to your life. When you establish positive relationships, it creates the opportunity for those relationships to have a positive influence on you; decreasing or eliminating any negativity you may face. Positive relationships offer an exchange of support and care, reduced stress and risk of depression, encouragement for healthy thinking and behavior, and the ability to heal a lot quicker. By building positive and supportive relationships, you will be happier and more satisfied with your life.

Purpose

Having a purpose is when you recognize that you belong and are meant for something bigger than yourself. Your purpose will shape your mindset and attitude, guide your decisions, and influence your feelings and behaviors. When you know your purpose, you know who you are, what you are, and why you are. You will find yourself living life with more integrity and being true to your morals and values. Having a healthy sense of purpose will help you to participate in things that give your life meaning. More importantly, you will be able to find meaning in the negative things you have experienced in life, and use those experiences to contribute to your post-traumatic growth.

These five pillars of resilience represent the focus areas that contribute to our growth mindset and overall well-being. Each pillar can be effective on its own, but in order to achieve optimal resilience, you must foster all five pillars together. After everything Black people have been through, and will go through moving forward, it's probably hard to see resilience as an effective solution or tool to overcome these challenges. Optimal resilience is not about avoiding stress or hardships, but rather knowing that these things are inevitable and learning to be successful in spite of it. Don't underestimate the power of resilience.

Processing Session

1. Have you ever suffered from depression? What were your signs of depression?

2. When you had depression, did you know? If so, what did you do in response to it and why?

3. Are you struggling with depression now? How do you know?

4. If you are struggling with depression, what are you doing to combat it? Is it working?

5. Thinking back, were you ever in a relationship with someone who was depressed and didn't realize it? What would you have done differently had you known then?

6. Moving forward, what will you do to ensure that you end the cycle of depression?

7. Does the concept of resiliency make sense? How do you think resiliency can help contribute to your well-being?

8. How do you plan to incorporate the 5 pillars of resiliency into your daily life? Which one do you think you would like to master first?

Chapter 10 Phases of Recovery

For individuals who have experienced different forms of trauma, the primary goal is recovery. Recovery doesn't mean complete freedom from the traumatic event, but the ability to live without constantly fighting the thoughts and feelings from the past. This process is also not quick and easy. Years of trauma cannot be undone on your own and in a matter of days. When you begin your road to recovery, you will want to do this with a trained mental health professional who can help guide you through each phase of recovery.

In her book *Trauma and Recovery*, Judith Herman presents a three-stage model that describes, in detail, the healing process for those suffering with the effects of trauma. The three phases of recovery are safety and stability, remembrance and mourning, and reconnection and integration. These stages are not at all linear. Depending on each individual person, you will move through each stage at your own pace, and possibly in a different order. Let's looks at this model more in-depth to see how it can help improve your overall quality of life.

Phase 1

Safety and Stability is the first phase of the recovery model. Being affected by trauma, you might feel unsafe in your body and in your relationships. In order to establish a sense of safety, you must understand what is causing you to feel unsafe. Let's recall in chapter 7, when the stress response system was discussed. It was explained that the brain has a natural alarm system (fight or flight) that goes off in times of true danger, but trauma can cause the brain's alarm system to malfunction. If someone has endured severe trauma or endured trauma over a period of time, the brain will no longer be able to tell the difference between real danger and perceived danger.

For example, let's say a woman named Terry experienced a rape when she was 16 by a man who wore a certain type of cologne. The scent of that cologne will remain present in her subconscious even in her adult life. Let's say one day she is out shopping for cologne with her boyfriend and all of sudden he sprays a cologne with same scent as the one her rapist wore. In this moment, she is reminded of the rape and her brain's alarm system is activated because it perceives danger. Her behavioral response might look like leaving abruptly or reacting with agitation, or even aggression. She isn't in danger, but her brain can't tell the difference. The goal of phase one would be to create safety and stability by calming her central nervous system; helping her to gain control of her fight or flight responses.

In phase one, you also create a sense of safety by building a strong support system; a safe place to live, financial security, mobility, and relationship support. Being affected by trauma, you might have developed trust issues. You may believe that everyone is out to get you, you can't depend on anyone, or that people will judge you. Building a strong support system starts the process of identifying individuals who can help support you on your road to recovery. People who you can trust to be there when you need them.

Phase 2

Remembrance and mourning is the second phase of the recovery model. This phase is a very emotional phase. The reason phase one establishes safety, is because phase two is where you begin to remember the traumatic events and process what happen. Referencing the safety phase will allow a person to move through phase two in hopes of not reacting to their fight or flight responses. There needs to be a balance with feeling safe and facing the past. This phase also involves the important task of exploring and mourning the losses associated with the traumatic event, and providing the opportunity to grieve. Most people may not realize this, but when you experience a trauma, you experience a loss that is similar to the death of a loved one. Grieving is essential in this phase, because the grieving process moves you towards acceptance.

In 1969, Elisabeth Kubler-Ross published her book, *On Death and Dying*, introducing the 5 stages of grief. The 5 stages of grief include, denial, anger, bargaining, depression, and acceptance. Just like the three phases aren't linear, neither are the 5 stages of grief. As you cycle through the 5 stages, the amount of time you spend in each stage will depend on you. When you are in the denial stage, you are in complete disbelief about the trauma/loss you've experienced. It's almost like you experience complete disassociation because the event was too much to handle. You suppress your emotions and pretend they don't exist.

For example, let's says a man named Trey gets locked up at age 25, and was sentenced to 5-10 years; a sentence that doesn't match the crime he committed. Even though Trey comes home with a plan, he is still having a hard time adjusting to the outside world. Things are not going as planned and all he can think about is all the years he has lost in prison. He is in complete disbelief at how much things have changed and how hard it is to come home and be successful. Being home was supposed to feel good, but the challenges he is facing are too much to handle. It's almost like he is still in prison, and he begins to withdraw into his own world.

When you are in the anger stage, you tend to have a hard time dealing with your real emotions. Anger is a secondary emotion, meaning when you express anger, it is not the actual emotion you feel. Think of it using the tip of the ice berg; the top would be the anger you express, but beneath the surface are the emotions you actually feel, but can't cope with. Emotions such as guilt, embarrassment, humiliation, anxiety, depression, fear, jealousy, rejection, insecurity, hurt, shame, and abandonment. For Trey, he is thinking, "This isn't fair!! I didn't deserve to be there for all those years! I was just trying to help my mom! I'm trying to do better, but no-one will give me a chance!". Trey may be expressing anger, but the emotions he is actually feeling are fear, rejection, and helplessness.

Although these stages are not linear, experiencing these wide range of emotions may transition you into the bargaining stage. When you are in the bargaining stage, you feel an overwhelming sense of helplessness. You begin to use "if only" statements in an attempt to gain some form of control. You focus more on what could have been done differently to have a different outcome. For Trey, these statements might sound like "If only I refused to be the driver," "If only I had fought harder to get out of prison sooner," "If only my father had been around to help out," or "If only my mom didn't get sick and lose her job." He might make promises to do better in exchange for favors. "God, if you help, I promise to do better and not go back to jail."

The depression stage represents the emptiness felt knowing a loved one is gone or the situation remains the same. In this stage, you might withdraw from everything you use to do, feel numb, or not want to get out of bed. You may also act out by being promiscuous, self-medicating with drugs or alcohol, or being reckless with your behavior. For Trey, he starts heavy drinking, being cold or harsh with his responses, refusing to leave the house, and when he does, he is seen hanging around the wrong people. To others, "See, I knew he ain't change. All those years in prison and he still ain't learn his lesson." The truth is that, Trey is depressed and struggling to hold on to what little hope he may have left. It's important for you and those around you to be able to recognize when you've become stuck in the depression stage. Remember, being depressed severely impacts the ability to be resilient and overcome the trauma you've experienced.

Acceptance is the final stage of the grief process, and it's considered a gift. There are a lot of people who never accept the loss and are therefore ruled by it. The process of grief has to be complete in order for someone to move on. Without fully expressing and embracing the emotions of the loss, it remains alive, as if it were constantly happening. The goal of this stage is to begin to heal and overcome the fear of the traumatic memories. Acceptance is an important part of the healing process in order to integrate these memories into your daily life. For Trey, acceptance looks like a complete attitude change. He begins to see things more clearly and speak more positively. He understands the concept of manifestation and is taking back the control over his life. He learns that he needs to evolve into his new reality and that acceptance may be a difficult road to take, but it is also a powerful one.

Phase 3

Reconnection and integration is the last phase of the recovery model. In this phase, you will achieve what's called post-traumatic growth (PTG); a positive change experienced as a result of the struggle with a traumatic event. It's about maintaining a sense of hope, knowing that you haven't just survived a trauma, but achieved overall life changes. PTG is reflected in strengthening your healthy relationships, increasing your personal strengths, and developing an awareness of the possibilities in life.

During the process of achieving PTG, you will desire and seek out healthier attachments with family, friends, and romantic partners. You will regain the ability to trust and will begin to restore relationships. If in a relationship during this time, you will become more aware of the unhealthiness you have contributed to the relationship and make amends. If you have children, you will recognize the ways in which your traumatic experiences have directly affected their development (ACEs), and take steps to prevent possible negative outcomes (toxic cycle). You will also regain the ability to feel in control while maintaining your healthy connections with others.

During this time, you will also be in the process of developing a new sense of self. You will find yourself identifying and focusing on your personal strengths in order to use them as catalysts for your well-being. Your well-being is directly affected by how happy you are. So, focusing on your strengths leads to higher levels of happiness and happiness improves your overall wellbeing. It has been said that the key to fulfillment is to recognize your core strengths. Your core strengths are skills that can help you to resolve problems and accomplish goals. Examples of some core strengths include discipline, patience, honesty, self-awareness, and perseverance. Once you have mastered the ability to focus and use your core strengths, a rewarding and fulfilling life will be sure to follow.

The last thing you will develop during this process are personal and professional goals that reflect PTG. You will transform your unwanted thoughts and feelings into positive actions. You will take everything you've experienced and integrate it into your daily life in order to continue to heal and grow. In other words, you will turn your pain into power. Examples of this include participating in walks or runs in order to raise awareness for diseases like cancer, lupus, or ALS. Reading self-help books or educating yourself in the area of your trauma to further help yourself and others. Starting a non-profit or a business in the name of a loved one you have lost. Keeping a written or virtual journal of your healing process or creating a blog/writing a book to help provide understanding and healing. No matter what path you choose, it will be a daily representation of your PTG.

The overall goal of the third phase is for you to develop a stable and permanent shift of mindset that is capable of ensuring your overall well-being in the long run. You will recognize the impact of your traumas and choose to take the necessary steps in moving towards empowerment and self-determination. It is important to know that it's not the trauma that defines your PTG, but what you are able to develop and foster from within yourself.

"You can't win the war against the world, if you can't win the war against your own mind"
-Will Smith

Processing Session

1. Why do you think healing is important for you?

2. In what ways would you need to make yourself safe and stable?

3. What traumas would you need to revisit and process through in order to reach acceptance?

4. Have your traumas affected others around you? If so, how?

5. Identify strengths that can help you with solving a problem or accomplishing a goal.

   a. What are you good at?

   b. What are you most complimented on?

   c. What brings you happiness?

6. In what ways can you turn your pain into power?

7. If you have already turned your pain into power, how can you encourage others to do the same?

8. Are you ready to start your healing process? If so, what is your plan to not only start but to stay committed to the process?

Epilogue

In this book, I have shared information to help resolve the disconnect between Black men and women, and it starts with YOU and your healing process. For far too long, we have blamed one another for the destruction between us, but now we know that we are all part of the problem. We all carry residue from our personal and collective pasts, and for most of us, that residue is the culprit behind the toxicity in our lives. We must take accountability for our part and put energy into ensuring that we don't continue to contribute to that toxicity. Only the healing of

Black mental health can end the cycle of unhealthy and toxic broken families within our communities.

Now that you have a pretty good road map of how to get to your healing process, the next step is to ensure that you understand how to use that to drive the reconnection. After I went through my healing process, I was so excited and ready to get out there and find my black man to love on. Unfortunately, I ran into not one, not two, but THREE unhealthy BM, and became a victim of emotional serial killers. #HealingProcessRedo.

During my real-life processing session, I realized, although I went through my healing process, I went back out into a world of unhealthy BM with my "dos" and "don'ts", but with no real solid plan. Of course, not all Black men are unhealthy, but the odds of running into one, or three in my case, is high. I realized that, in order to be successful, having a plan was going to be essential before I decided to get back out there and try again. #PostTraumaticGrowth

Once you've accomplished your version of post-traumatic growth, you will have freed yourself from the trauma drama that plagued your life and relationships. You will create a healthy space where you no longer tell yourself, "I don't need a man" or "this is too good to be true." You will finally be in a place where you can either better the relationship you are in or begin to focus on finding that "4th type of person to let in your car." Ladies, you can focus on finding a healthy BM that makes you feel safe and secure when he takes the lead in your life. Fellas, you can focus on finding a healthy BW that creates a stress-free environment and gives the type of support you need to feel like the man in her life. Either way, before you decide to go back out there and try again, you will also need a plan; and that plan is called dating with a purpose.

Dating with a PURPOSE

Practice Patience

Have you ever dated someone and a couple of months later you say to yourself "This is not the same person I met before" or "What do we really have in common?" That's because a lot of us don't take adequate time to get to know the person we are dating. Take the time to have open and honest conversations. Have discussions about topics such as

- Upbringing (childhood, education, ect.)
- Family dynamics
- Healing from trauma? (Resiliency/PTG)
- Personality (similarities and differences)
- Morals, Values, and Character
- Friendships of the opposite sex
- The five love languages
- Apology languages
- Reading and having discussions
- Parenting styles or if you even want kids
- Gender roles
- Bank Account (separate, joint, ect.)
- Financial literacy (Generational Wealth)
- Spirituality beliefs
- Marriage or Not
- Living Will
- Living together before marriage or not
- To be or not to be Monogamous
- Sexual Compatibility
- Short and long-term goals
- Communications skills (triggers, conflict resolution skills, coping skills, compromising skills, emotional intelligence ect.)

The goal is to have more meaningful conversations in order to determine true compatibility and connection. You are building the foundation of your relationship when you are dating. If your foundation is weak, then your relationship will crumble. Ensure that your foundation can sustain the relationship for the long-term.

Universal Law of Attraction

Everything we experience in life is dictated by our mindset. Our mindset is the most powerful weapon we have; it can either create or destroy. The emotional energy you put out is what you will get back. So, focus all your emotional and mental energy on everything your heart desires, in order to attract it into your life. Always speak your dreams into existence; walk, talk, and live like it already exists, and eventually it will.

Resiliency

Respect the process. Understand that just because you're healthy doesn't mean you will magically find "the one." It takes work, and that means sifting through the unhealthy ones to find your healthy one. Don't allow the unhealthy experiences to steal your desire to be in a relationship. Take time to self-reflect in order to overcome those dating challenges. Remember, in order to achieve optimal resilience, you must foster all five pillars together. Don't underestimate the power of resilience.

Protect your Peace

Always make sure you use self-care during relationships. Energy is transferable. Never allow the unhealthiness of another individual to toxify your energy. You come first. Secure your happiness by focusing on your strengths, doing things that bring you joy, and speaking positive affirmations. Speaking positive affirmations in the morning or listening to them while you sleep will not only bring you success, but also protect you from the negativity of others. If you ever find yourself questioning whether or not to move on from the person you are dating, ask yourself these three questions. Is this situation;

- Safe
- Beneficial
- Healthy

If the answer to these questions is NO, then it's time to GO.

Only ONE

It has been said that you should date multiple people at once so that you don't put all your eggs in one basket and waste time if it doesn't work out. In my humble opinion, this would be counter-productive to what you are trying to accomplish. Your goal is to build a strong foundation that will lead to a long-lasting relationship. How can you accomplish the goal of truly getting to know someone when your attention is spread amongst multiple people? Additionally, if you have the understanding that the odds of meeting an unhealthy individual is high, why allow the opportunity for multiple unhealthy people to be in your space at once? Instead, focus on getting to know one person, and allow your growth to do its job. Remember, the new you will crave healthier relationships, and therefore you will be more likely to recognize and disassociate from the unhealthy energy of others.

Sex can wait

This ties in with practicing patience. When you are taking the time to get to know someone, make a conscious commitment to maintain abstinence. Some may think sex is the foundation of a relationship, or that it is important to build chemistry, but in fact, it is the other way around. When you decide to engage in sexual activity prematurely, it clouds your judgement, intensifies your emotions, and/or creates emotions that you didn't have initially. Waiting allows you to build genuine intimacy, chemistry, and a strong organic healthy connection with the right person. Remember, energy is transferable. When you engage in sexual activity, you are exchanging sexual energy. Be careful who you allow in your space. Your body is your temple, governed by your energy; protect it.

Evolve

The healing process is never-ending; you will always need to overcome a challenge and heal. Too often, we jump from one situation to another without taking time to process what happened. When a relationship doesn't work out, ensure that you are not carrying old baggage into a new relationship. Take the time to self-reflect, process, heal, and evolve before trying again. There is always a lesson to be learned and growth to be made.

I hope that those reading this book found it to be as helpful and impactful as I intended it to be. I hope this book allowed you to have amazing and fulfilling inner monologue, and/or dialogue

amongst friends, family and social media plat-
forms. I am extremely passionate about self-re-
flection and growth, so I welcome any feedback
at royaltyretreatment@gmail.com. Thank you for
your love and support. You are greatly appreciated.

-Queen

Acknowledgements

I would like to acknowledge and thank all the Black men that not only supported and encouraged me through my entire writing process, but also for providing me with all of the necessary data needed to write this book. I could not have done it without you.

References

Books

Alexander, M. (2010). *The new Jim Crow: Mass incarceration in the age of colorblindness.* The New Press.

Ali, S. (1989). *The Blackman's Guide to Understanding the Blackwoman.* Shahrazad Ali

Herman, Judith Lewis. *Trauma and Recovery.* New York, NY : Basic Books, 1992. Print.

Kubler-Ross, E. (1970). *On death and dying.* Collier Books/Macmillan Publishing Co.

Leary, Joy DeGruy. *Post Traumatic Slave Syndrome: America's Legacy of Enduring Injury and Healing.* Milwaukie, Oregon: Uptone Press, 2005.

Perry, B. D., & Szalavitz, M. (2008). *The Boy who was Raised as a Dog: And other stories from a child psychiatrist's notebook: what traumatized children can teach us about loss, love, and healing.* New York: Basic Books.

Szalavitz, M., & Perry, B. D. (2010). *Born for love: Why empathy is essential-- and endangered.* New York: William Morrow.

Films

Ava Duvernay & Jason Moran. (2016) *13th*

D. Channsin Berry, Bill Duke. (2011) *Dark Girls*

Videos

Black Angel Media. (2017, April 26) *The Secret Meeting That Changed Rap Music and Destroyed a Generation* [Video]. www.youtube.com

Chicago Humanities Festival. (2011, Dec 14). *Bruce D. Perry: Social & Emotional Development in Early Childhood* [Video]. www.youtube.com

DrugPolicyAlliance. (2016, Sept 15). *Jay Z –The War on Drugs: From Prohibition to Gold Rush* [Video]. www.youtube.com

DJ Vlad. (2016, Oct 5). *Dr. Umar Johnson Talks America's War Against Black Men* [Video]. www.youtube.com

Early Years Scotland. (2017, Nov 16). *Dr Bruce Perry-Early Brain Development: Reducing the Effects of Trauma* [Video]. www.youtube.com

I.A. Lewis. (2016, April 6). *The Willie Lynch Letter and the making of slave* [Video]. www.youtube.com

TED. (2015, Feb 17) *How childhood trauma effects health across a lifetime/Nadine Burke Harris* [Video]. www.youtube.com

Reelblack. (2019, Nov 19). *The Blackman's Guide to Understanding the Black Woman (1991). | Shahrazad Ali* [Video]. www.youtube.com

Terrance Carney. (2016, Sept 12). *Dr. Joy DeGruy Leary: Post Traumatic Slave Syndrome* [Video]. www.youtube.com

Websites

Anand, T. (2018, April 24). *"A Brief Summary of The First Wave of Feminism"*. Feminism in India. www.feminisminindia.com/

Anand, T. (2018, April 25). *A Brief Summary of The Second Wave of Feminism.* Feminism in India. www.feminisminindia.com/

Bounce Back Project. (n.d). *Resilience.* www.bounce-backproject.org

Carten, A. (2016, August 22). *The Racist Roots of Welfare Reform*. The New Republic. www.newrepublic.com

History Editors. (2009, October 29). *Great Depression History*. www.history.com

History Editors. (2018, February 28). *Jim Crow Laws*. www.history.com

History Editors. (2018, August 21). *Just Say No*. www.history.com

National Child Traumatic Stress Network. (n.d.). *Trauma types*. www.nctsn.org

National Center for Disease and Control (2020, April 13): *Adverse Childhood Experiences (ACEs)*. www.cdc.gov/

Paul, C. A. (2017). *The New Deal*. https://socialwelfare.library.vcu.edu

Pilgrim, Dr. D. (2012, August). *The Sapphire Caricature*. www.ferris.edu

Articles

Clark, K. B. (1940) "*Skin color as a factor in racial identification of Negro school children.*" J. of Social Psychology 11: 169-178.

Elizabeth Hinton, LeShae Henderson, and Cindy Reed. *An Unjust Burden: The Disparate Treatment of Black Americans in the Criminal Justice System.* New York: Vera Institute of Justice, 2018

Equal Justice Initiative, "*Reconstruction in America: Racial Violence after the Civil War, 1865-1876*" (2020). www.eji.org

Fontaine, N. (2011, May 5). "*From Mammy to Madea, and Examination of the Behaviors of Tyler Perry's Madea Character in Relation to the Mammy, Jezebel, and Sapphire Stereotypes.* www. scholarworks.gsu.edu

Grimlich, J. (2020, May 6). *Black imprisonment rate in the U.S. has fallen by a third since 2006.* www.pewresearch.org

Kenneth J. Neubeck and Noel Cazenave (2003) "*Welfare Racism: Playing the Race Card Against America's Poor..,*" The Journal of Sociology & Social Welfare: Vol. 30 : Iss. 1 , Article 21

Libby Nelson & Dara Lind (2015, February 24). *The school to prison pipeline, explained.* www.justicepolicy.org

Robbins, W. (1981, August 15). *Philadelphia suffers in Manufacturing Job Exodus.* New York Times. p. 6. www.nytimes.com

Trina Jones & Kimberly Jade Norwood, *Aggressive Encounters & White Fragility: Deconstructing the Trope of the Angry Black Woman,* 5 IOWA L. REV.102 (2017)

U.S. Department of Labor, Bureau of Labor Statistics. (1990). *Prisoners in 1989.* (BLS Bulletin No. 2700) www.bjs.gov

World Federation for Mental Health. (2012). *Depression: A Global Crisis*

Made in the USA
Columbia, SC
02 January 2021

30165643R00124